均衡飲食
低膽固醇食譜

LOW-CHOLESTEROL
CHINESE CUISINE

本書係與中國文化大學建教合作出版

作　　者：鄧昭昭・陳雪霞

設　　計：汪金光・張方馨

策　　劃：邱澄子

封面設計：
照　　相：洛奇攝影有限公司

翻　　譯：戴海蒂

協助人員：王櫻閣・陳素眞・張麗雯

　　　　　賴燕眞・李淑慧・邱淑琦

Author: Teng Chao Chao, Chen Hsueh Hsia
Designer: Wang Chin-Kuang, Fandra Chang
Planner: Cheng-Tzu Chiu
Cover Designer
Photographer : Logi Design & Photograph LTD.
Translator: Heidi Dick
Collaborators: Wang Ying-Kuo, Chen Su-Jen
　　　　　　　Chang Li-Wen, Lai Yen-Jen
　　　　　　　Li Su-Huei, Shirley Chiu

製版：喬茂印刷製版有限公司

序 INTRODUCTION

近幾年來，國內十大死亡原因由營養不良導向的傳染性疾病，轉移爲營養過多的文明病，這是生活富裕、享受口腹之慾所帶來的隱憂。爲免於遭受文明病的侵擾，除正常作息、經常性運動外，最重要的還是從"均衡飲食"做起；如此不但能安然品嚐各種佳餚美食，更能永保健康。

"均衡飲食"不僅是健康的基石，而且是保健的不二法門。任何病痛以其爲藍本，只要配合身體狀況來調節飲食中的一種或多種營養素，或改變熱能，或變化質地，或調整風味，或增減份量及餐次，即能獲得改善。有了均衡飲食的營養觀念，不管是高蛋白質飲食或低脂肪飲食，都可依其原則靈活運用，以符合身體健康的需要。

本書不僅介紹護身符"均衡飲食"，也對威脅生命的膽固醇有所敍述，以達預防勝於治療。除各篇依五大類食物分別有數段有益健康的精要說明外，食譜均屬家常菜，製作簡單，且附有主要營養素的成份表，讀者可觸類旁通廣泛運用，使每日飲食富於變化，掌握"均衡"的原則，而無後顧之憂。

本書能如期付梓，承蒙 味全出版社鼎力協助，本系林主任支持，王助教櫻閣及多位學生的幫忙，特此申謝。

鄧昭昭、陳雪霞共識

One of the ten major causes of death in Taiwan used to be contagious diseases resulting from malnutrition. Yet during recent years, this trend has shifted to death caused by excessive consumption of certain nutrients. For along with prosperity enjoyed during modern times come the lurking dangers arising from fulfilling the desires of the palate. In order to avoid suffering from this 'modern-day disease', besides one's daily routine and regular exercise, the most important foundation of health is still a well-balanced diet.

A balanced diet is not just the base on which one's health is established but is also the only route to its sustenance. As the blueprint to good health, a variety of nutritional adjustments can improve one's health as long as they are coordinated with one's physiological needs. For example, one can regulate one or many nutrients in one's diet, change the caloric intake, vary the texture of food, adjust the flavor, or increase/decrease the portions and frequency of meals. With the nutritional concept of a balanced diet, one can actively utilize such changes in the diet to meet the requirements of the individual.

This book not only introduces the amulet known as a balanced diet, but also includes safeguards against life-threatening cholesterol. In this way, it is hoped that readers adopt the nutritional theory of "prevention is better than cure".

The book includes sections that provide essential nutritional explanations which are divided according to the five major food groups and are designed to benefit one's health. The recipes in this book are classified as home-style dishes which are simple to make and accompanied by essential nutritional content. By grasping the principles of "Low-Cholesterol Chinese Cuisine", the readers can make inferences from the recipes to make daily meals rich in variety.

We are much indebted to Wei Chuan Publishing Co's exceptional assistance in the prompt publication of this book. We would like to give special thanks to Lin Sui Yi, the Chairperson of our department, Assistant Professor Wang Ying Kuo, as well as many students.

Teng Chao Chao , Chen Hsueh Hsia

編著簡歷　AUTHOR BACKGROUND

鄧昭昭：中國文化大學食品營養系副教授，擔任營養學、膳食療養課程。
著　作：「幼兒營養問題之研究」、「營養與健康」等。
陳雪霞：中國文化大學食品營養系講師，擔任食物製備課程。
著　作：「速簡食譜」、「中華文化餐飲圖譜」等。

Teng Chao Chao:
Assistant Professor, Food and Nutrition Department of Chinese Culture University. Teaches classes in Nutrition and Dietary Curing/Disease Treatment.
Publications: 'Study of Infant Nutrition Problems', 'Nutrition and Health', etc.

Chen Hsueh Hsia:
Lecturer, Food and Nutrition Department of Chinese Culture University. Teaches Food Preparation Classes.
Publications: 'Quick and Easy Recipes', 'Simple, Traditional Chinese Recipes'.

目 錄 TABLE OF CONTENTS

● 備註   **Note**

■書內之菜餚為方便讀者應用，在本目錄以不同色符標示，食譜應用方法請參照第10頁。

■The recipes in this cookbook have been color coded for your convenience according to meal type. Please refer to P.10 for directions on how to use this color coded system to plan meals.

■葷菜 Meat/Fish Dishes ■半葷菜 Meat/Fish/Vegetable Dishes ■蔬菜 Vegetable Dishes
■湯 Soups   早餐 Breakfasts   ■午餐 Lunchs

健康益壽之道～均衡飲食

均衡飲食是保持健康的良好方法。所謂均衡飲食就是每日五大類食物均需攝取，且質量適宜。

人的一生由胎兒到老年期，除嬰兒前四～六個月全靠嬰兒奶外，其他時間都要仰賴五穀及根莖類／肉、魚、豆、蛋、奶／油脂／蔬菜／水果等五大類食物，所不同的只是量的差異；且每餐最好包括五類，使所有營養素均在，因為沒有任何一種食物包含所有營養素，也沒有一種營養素能單獨執行功能，必須配合其他營養素來輔助，才能達成任務。

人體若因飲食攝取不足或偏食而缺乏一種或多種營養素，生理功能就會受到牽制或阻擾，容易產生疲倦、體重不足、虛弱多病的現象。反之，攝取過多，對身體亦將產生不良影響；如蛋白質、醣、脂肪等熱能營養素（米麵、肉類、甜點等）吸收過量，可能造成肥胖，引發退化性疾病─糖尿病、心臟病、動脈硬化、腎臟病、高血壓、中風，甚至癌症等；而維生素或礦物質（如魚肝油、維生素丸）攝取過多，則可能中毒並產生各種病痛。因此飲食的過與不足均屬不當，如何才能吃得恰到好處呢？關鍵之鑰就是均衡飲食。

THE WAY TO HEALTH AND LONGEVITY～

A BALANCED DIET

A balanced diet is one of the keys to good health. A 'balanced diet' means getting the proper amount and quality of each of the five food groups every day.

Besides the first four to six months of human life when we are dependent solely upon milk as a source of nutrition, we require a diet consisting of grains, root-stock, milk, eggs, meats, fish, beans, fats, vegetables and fruits. The only variable is the amount each individual requires at certain stages in life. Each meal should include food items from all five groups. There is no one type of food which contains all the necessary nutrients. Therefore, all of the different food groups must work as spokes of a synergetic wheel.

If there is not enough of a certain nutrient due to an imbalanced diet or finicky eating habits, the body's normal functions suffer as a consequence. This often leads to fatigue, excessive weight loss and weakness. Absorbing too much of certain nutrients can have deleterious effects. Overconsumption of foods high in protein, carbohydrates, and fat (rice noodles, meats, desserts, etc.) can cause obesity as well as degenerative diseases such as diabetes, hypertension, arteriosclerosis, kidney disease, heart disease, apoplexy, and even cancer. Excessive consumption of vitamins and minerals in the form of cod-liver oil or vitamin tablets is also harmful, and may cause various complications.

Therefore, we should not consume too much or too little of certain foods in the diet. How do we know we are getting the right foods? The key is a balanced diet.

五大類食物及均衡飲食

我國行政院衛生署依食物的功能及成人每日所需營養素攝取量,將五大類食物份量分配如下表,讀者可參考運用,同時本書第120、121頁食物代換表並有每一類相等營養價值的數種食物可供代換,不僅讓您享受口腹之慾,並可達到均衡的效果。

五大類食物飲食指南 (成人每日用量)

食物類別	份量	份量單位說明
五穀及根莖類	3～6份 註1	每份/飯一碗(200公克)或中型饅頭一個或土司麵包4片 ■依個人熱能的需要增減,最好能攝取含纖維、維生素及礦物質的胚芽米或糙米。
肉、魚、豆、蛋、奶類	5份	每份/*牛奶或豆漿一杯(240 cc)/*蛋一個 /肉、家禽或魚類熟重30公克/豆腐一塊(100公克) *記號為每日食用一份,其餘可每日變換。
油脂類	3大匙	每匙/15公克,為塗在麵包及炒菜用。
蔬菜類	3份	每份/蔬菜約100公克 ■每日至少一份富含維生素A的深綠、深黃紅色類蔬菜如菠菜、紅蘿蔔等。
水果類	2份	每份/中型鮮果一個(100公克) ■每日至少一份含維生素C量多的水果,如柳丁、葡萄柚、柑橘、番茄或蕃石榴等。

■各類食物宜選用當地各季節盛產的為佳。

註1 在其他四大類食物份量不變的情況下,3～6份的五穀根莖類攝取量所產生的總熱能差異為:

  3份－1831卡 4份－2103卡 5份－2375卡 6份－2647卡,讀者確定個人所需熱能(請參考第10頁)後,可依此決定攝取五穀根莖類份數。

THE FIVE FOOD GROUPS AND A BALANCED DIET

The National Health Administration of the Executive Yuan has categorized the appropriate portions of the five food groups in the following table according to the functions of various foods and recommended daily nutritional allowances. Readers are encouraged to use the table as a source of reference. Also, the food exchange table on pages 120 and 121 provides the nutritional values for every type of food so that you can both satisfy your palate and achieve balanced, healthy results.

Food Group Dietary Guide (daily allowances for adults)

Food group	Portion	Note
Grains and root-stocks	3-6 portions (see note 1)	1 portion/one bowl of rice (1/2 1b. or 200g.) or one medium-sized piece of steamed bread or four pieces of toast. ■ according to the increase or decrease in the individual's caloric requirements. It's best if one can make germinated rice or unpolished rice a part of one's diet as both contain fiber, vitamins, and minerals.
Meat, Fish, Beans, Eggs, Milk	5 portions	1 portion/＊one cup of milk/＊one cup of soybean milk /＊ one egg/30g. (cooked weight) meat, poultry or fish/one square (1/4 1b. or 100g.) of bean curd. ＊ mark means that one portion should be consumed daily. Portions of others can be varied day to day.
Oils and fats	3 tablespoons	1 Tablespoon equals 1/2 oz. (15 g.), either spread on sliced bread (toast) or used for stir-frying.
Vegetables	3 portions	1 portion/about 1/4 1b. (100g.) vegetables ■ one portion of yellow, green vegetables daily, such as spinach and carrots which are rich in Vitamin A.
Fruits	2 portions	1 portion/one medium-sized fresh fruit (1/4 1b. or 100 g.) ■ at least one portion of fruit which contains a high volume of Vitamin C such as oranges, grapefruit, tangarines, tomatoes, or guavas, etc.

■ All foods should be chosen according to local seasons.

Note 1 As long as the portions of the other four food groups don't change, the differences in calories produced by the consumption of between 3-6 portions of the grains/root-stock group are as follows: 3 portions = 1831 cal. 4 portions = 2103 cal. 5 portions = 2375 cal. 6 portions = 2647 cal.

After determining your own caloric requirements (please refer to page 10), you can decide your individual daily allowance of grains/root-stocks accordingly.

認識膽固醇 RECOGNIZING CHOLESTEROL

人步入中年後，稍不留意，就容易發福；尤其現在社會經濟繁榮，生活安逸，活動量日漸減少，加上豐富的飲食，膽固醇及血脂肪很容易在體內堆積過量，導致動脈硬化、心臟病等心血管疾病而危及健康，因此平時的飲食務必注意膽固醇的攝取。

膽固醇是一種脂肪，它在我們身體每一個細胞膜上都有，尤其是腦、腎上腺、肝及周圍神經含量最多。此外，膽固醇也是製造維生素 D、膽汁、性賀爾蒙及腎上腺皮質賀爾蒙等的主要成份。維生素 D 可以促進鈣質的吸收及利用；膽汁則可幫助脂肪及脂溶性維生素的吸收；而賀爾蒙不僅是所有營養素新陳代謝所必須，更是進行人體生理作用所必備的物質。

膽固醇的來源有二，其一是食用動物性食物所含的膽固醇，一般人每日約可攝取 500 到 800 毫克；其二爲不含膽固醇，但含有蛋白質、醣類及脂肪的食物，均可在體內轉變爲膽固醇，此製造量約爲 1000 到 2000 毫克，若飲食熱能的攝取合於個人的需要，則飲食中的膽固醇與身體所製造的膽固醇互有補償作用。但熱能攝取量超過個人需要量時，身體製造的膽固醇量仍不會少於 1000 毫克，因此飲食來源的膽固醇就容易滯留在血液中，形成血脂過高的情形。

爲了預防膽固醇過高，每日食物中膽固醇的攝取應低於 400 毫克，不僅要限制含高量膽固醇的食物，更應避免攝取過多米飯、麵食、甜點等含有蛋白質、醣類及脂肪的食物。

謹將各類食物每 100 公克所含膽固醇量簡列於右：

After we reach middle age, it's easy to become overweight. This is especially true in an economically prosperous society where lifestyles are more stable and the amount of movement we experience each day is steadily decreasing. Moreover, with a rich diet, excessive amounts of cholesterol and fat are easily trapped in the body. This leads to arteriosclerosis, hypertension and other ailments. Therefore, it is necessary to monitor one's cholesterol intake.

Cholesterol is a type of fat. It exists in every cell membrane of the human body. Cells of the brain, adrenal glands, liver and nervous system contain the largest amounts. Moreover, cholesterol produces Vitamin D, bile, sex hormones, adrenocortical hormones, and other secretions found in the body. Vitamin D serves as a catalyst in the absorption and use of calcium. Bile assists in the absorption of fats and fat-soluble vitamins. Hormones are not only necessary in the metabolism of all nutrients in the body but are needed for the general physiological functions and processes in the body.

There are two sources of cholesterol, one of which is found in meats, fish, and poultry. The average person can absorb 500-800 milligrams daily. The second source of cholesterol is food that does not contain cholesterol itself, but contains protein, carbohydrates, and fat. These may be transformed into cholesterol in the body at a rate of 1000 to 2000 milligrams per day. If the caloric content in the diet is sufficient, then the cholesterol in the diet and the cholesterol produced naturally in the body complement one another. But when the caloric content in the diet exceeds that which is needed, cholesterol is still produced in the body at a rate of at least 1000 mg. per day. Therefore, the cholesterol obtained from the diet is easily trapped in the blood and becomes a source of excess fat in the bloodstream.

To avoid overconsumption of cholesterol, the cholesterol content in the diet should be kept below 400 mg. per day. Not only should consumption of foods high in cholesterol content be limited, but foods high in protein , carbohydrates, and fat—such as rice, noodles, and desserts-should be consumed in moderation as well.

A cholesterol content chart for various food groups based on 3-1/2 oz. Servings is shown on page 9.

膽固醇含量表 CHOLESTEROL CONTENT CHART

食物名稱 Food Group	毫克 (mg.)	食物名稱 Food Group	毫克 (mg.)	食物名稱 Food Group	毫克 (mg.)
五穀類 Grains	0	鴨肉 Duck	64	鮑魚 Abalone	182
蔬菜類 Vegetables	0	豬肉 Pork	67	鰻魚 Eel	189
水果類 Fruits	0	雞肉 Chicken	75	蛤、蠔 Clams, Oysters	200
豆製類 Beans	0	蟹 Crab	80	豬肝、豬腰 Pig Liver, Pig Kidney	250
植物油 Vegetable Oil	0	牛肉 Beef	91	豬心 Pig Heart	274
蛋白 Egg Whites	0	羊肉、火腿 Lamb, Ham	100	魚卵 Fish Eggs	360
脫脂奶 Skim Milk	2	鯧魚、乳酪 Ribbonfish, Yogurt	120	蜆 Mussels	454
鮮奶 Whole Milk	12	沙丁魚 Sardines	140	雞蛋（2個） 2 Eggs	500
魚肉製品 Fish Meat Products	40	干貝 Scallops	145	乾魷魚 Dried Cuttlefish	615
一般海水魚 Fish	50～60	豬肚、豬腸、蝦 Tripe, Chitterlings, Shrimp	150	豬腦 Pig Brain	3000
一般淡水魚 Fresh Water Fish	60～80	章魚 Octopus	173		
香腸 Sausage	60	墨魚 Squid	180		

□綠色標記：低膽固醇食物，可任意食用。
□黃色標記：中膽固醇食物，尚可吃，但請稍加節制食用。
▨紅色標記：高膽固醇食物，中老年人及輕度工作者不宜多吃，幼少壯者不在此限。

□ **Green:** Zero to low cholesterol content. No consumption limit.
□ **Yellow:** Medium cholesterol content. Moderate consumption advised.
▨ **Red:** High cholesterol content. Not recommended for middle-aged people, the elderly, or people with low daily physical exertion levels.

均衡與低膽固醇飲食菜單範例與應用

RECIPE EXAMPLES AND USES FOR A BALANCED, LOW CHOLESTEROL DIET

本食譜之設計以行政院衛生署建議的國人飲食指南爲藍本，以均衡飲食爲第一原則，菜餚屬家常菜，供應熱能則以 2300 卡（±50 卡）註2 及膽固醇低於 400 毫克註3 爲依據，份量可供 4 人食用，不論體重過重（輕）或工作量較輕（重）者，均可自行減少（增加）1－2 碗飯、麵或點心來調整，若男士所需的熱能較高，尚可酌情再增加一份肉類或半葷素類及蔬果以符合需要。　　　　　註2：參考第7頁註1　　　　註3：參考第9頁膽固醇含量表

The 'Taiwan Dietary Guide', recommended by the National Health Administration of the Executive Yuan, serves as the blueprint for this cookbook. The most important principle in "Low-Cholesterol Chinese Cuisine" is a balanced diet.

The meals are home-style dishes and each provides approximately 2300 Calories (plus or minus 50 Cal.) (see note 2) and a cholesterol level which falls below 400 mg. (see page 9). Each dish serves four persons regardless of its weight or whether it's consumed by those with low or high levels of daily physical exertion. In order to make adjustments, one can either reduce or add 1-2 bowls of rice, noodles, or snacks. If a male's caloric requirements are higher, one might consider increasing one meat portion, a meat/vegetable portion, or a fruit/vegetable portion to meet his requirements.　　　　　Note 2: See Note 1 on P. 7

成人每日熱能建議攝取量 Suggested daily caloric intake for adults:

性別 Sex	年齡 Age	熱能 （卡） Calories		
		輕度工作 Low Level	中度工作 Med. Level	重度工作 High Level
男 M	20 歲以上　20 yrs. +	2400	2750	3250
	35 歲以上　35 yrs. +	2300	2650	3100
	55 歲以上　55 yrs. +	2000	2300	2700
女 F	20 歲以上　20 yrs. +	1950	2050	2250
	35 歲以上　35 yrs. +	1850	1950	2150
	55 歲以上　55 yrs. +	1650	1750	

輕度工作：如閱讀、打字及文書等。　　**中度工作：**稍需用力者，如拖地、打臘、木工等。
重度工作：如礦工、伐木工或跳舞及網球運動。讀者欲知熱能營養素之計算法可參考第 120 頁附表。

Low Level: studying, typing, and writing, etc.
Medium Level: requires slight physical effort, such as mopping, waxing, carpentry, etc.
High Level: mining, lumberjacking, dancing, tennis playing, etc.
If readers wish to know calculations of nutrients and calories, they can refer to the chart on page 120.

本食譜之應用原則

1. 本書內之菜餚分爲 ■葷菜 ▨半葷菜 ▨蔬菜 ▨湯 ▨早餐 ▨午餐，爲方便讀者應用；各類菜餚在目錄頁均以不同色符標示，讀者可任意選用同色符的菜餚替換。

2. 午餐爲節約時間，以簡餐型式設計，請再任選或自行調製一道湯配合食用，方才符合所設計的午餐營養要求（麵片湯及肉糠米粉除外）

3. 晚餐以供應三菜一湯爲原則，即葷、半葷、蔬菜及湯；忙碌時亦不妨選擇簡餐，祇要再酌加肉類、油脂及蔬菜各 2 份（份量請參考第 6 頁五大類食物飲食指南），其營養份就與晚餐相當。若工作量不大或想減肥者，則不必再添加任何食物，其營養也足夠供給身體所需。

4. 三餐熱能依比例分配約爲早餐 25％，午餐 35％，晚餐 40％，讀者也可依實際情況調整餐別的份量，祇要三餐總熱能符合個人每日所需即可。
菜餚千變萬化，最簡便的方法是讀者祇需依五大類食物飲食指南原則來變化自己喜愛的菜餚，即可達均衡的目的，或可參考第 120 頁食物代換表選用具有相同營養價值的食物經常替換，以增加菜餚的變化。

5. 所有食物材料均以除去廢棄部份並清洗後之淨重爲準。茲舉三日菜單範例供讀者參考運用：

1. The meals in this cookbook are divided into the following categories: meat/fish dishes, vegetable dishes, meat/fish/vegetable dishes, soups, and one-dish meals. One-dish meals are served as breakfast or lunch according to the differences in nutrients and serving portions.

2. In order to save time when preparing lunch, make one-dish meals and choose any soup (except Pork And Fish Paste Over Rice Noodles and Noodle Slice Soup) to accompany the dish.

3. The conventional dinner includes three dishes and one soup: A meat/fish dish, a vegetable dish, a meat/fish/vegetable dish, and a soup. When busy, it is easier to choose a one-dish meal by adding 2 portions each of meat, oil/fat, and vegetable (please refer to the five groups dietary guide on page 7 for the portions). The nutritional portions for this dish are the same as those for the conventional dinner. If your level of daily physical exertion is not high or you want to lose weight, you need not add any foods to this simple dish. The nutrients contained in the dish are sufficient in fulfilling bodily requirements.

4. The calories which comprise one's three meals are distributed according to the following ratio method : breakfast 25%, lunch 35%, dinner 40%. You can also adjust meal portions according to preference as long as the caloric total for all three meals is in line with your daily nutritional requirements. Dishes can be varied in many ways, the most easy and convenient of which is for you to change preferred dishes according to the principles established in the five food groups guide. In this way you can achieve a balanced objective. You can also refer to the food conversion table (page 120) and substitute dishes on a regular basis with those foods which have the same nutritional value.

5. The standard weighing of foods follows the discarding of unneeded parts and the washing of edible parts. The following three-day meals recommendation chart is included for your reference.

三日菜單範例　Recipes for three days

	例 一　Example 1	例 二　Example 2	例 三　Example 3
早餐	饅頭 1 個 荷包蛋 1 個 熟青菜 50 公克 豆漿 1 杯	土司 4 片 火腿（或熱狗）30 公克 奶油(或美奶滋)1 ½小匙 番茄、小黃瓜 50 公克 牛奶 1 杯	稀飯 2 碗 肉鬆 15 公克 豆腐 100 公克 炒熟青菜 50 公克
午餐	肉糠米粉 p.28	五彩涼麵 p.23 湯（任選）	咖哩炒飯 p.17 湯（任選）
晚餐	清蒸魚 p.74 海帶捲 p.49 素炒青花菜 p.104 雪花牛肉羹 p.66	吉利雞柳 p.32 雙色烘蛋 p.101 素炒高麗菜芽 p.107 四菇鮮湯 p.61	通心麵沙拉 p.25 湯（任選）
Breakfast:	1 piece of steamed bread 1 fried egg 1-3/4 oz. (50 g). cooked green vegetable 1 cup of soybean milk	4 pieces of toast 1 oz. (30 g.) ham (or hot dog) 1-1/2 t. butter (or mayonnaise) 50 g. tomato, gherkin cucumber one cup of milk	2 bowls congee 15 g. shredded pork 100 g. bean curd 50 g. stir-fried green vegetable
Lunch:	Pork And Fish Paste Over Rice Noodles	Cold Rainbow Noodles Soup (choose any)	Curry Fried Rice Soup (choose any)
Dinner:	Steamed Fish Seaweed Pork Rolls Stir-fried Broccoli Egg-White Beef And Spinach Soup	Breaded Chicken Breast Two Color Omelet Stir-Fried Cabbage Sprouts Chicken With Assorted Mushrooms Soup	Chinese Style Macaroni Salad Soup (choose any)

（本食譜之設計均為 4 人份，上列早餐範例欄中僅列 1 人份）

The recipes in this cookbook are designed for 4 person servings. However, the above breakfast meals list only 1 person portions.

五穀根莖類 GRAINS AND ROOTSTOCKS

稻米、小麥、大麥、燕麥、黑麥、玉米等均屬穀物；根莖類則包括馬鈴薯、蕃薯、芋頭、荸薺等等。五穀根莖類食物所供給的營養素主要是蛋白質、醣及熱能，而其中最豐富的首推醣類。

1.保持腦力的來源可不能少喲！

腦部組織的運作靈活必須仰賴血液不斷地供給葡萄糖。持續且嚴重的血糖過低，如過度的節食或飢餓，會使腦部受損且不易恢復。而體內葡萄糖的唯一來源為貯存肝臟的肝醣，因數量有限不敷使用(只有100公克)，必須由食物中攝取，也就是由含醣類較多的五穀根莖類食物來維持整個中樞神經的功能。所以工作上須經常用腦的人及學生，五穀根莖類的攝取更不容忽視。

2.如何防止疲勞使精力充沛

熱能是供給體力及活力的泉源。醣類製造熱能比較快速，脂肪供給的熱能則比較多。然而缺乏醣，脂肪不但不會氧化產生熱能，還會製造較多的酮體(脂肪氧化不完全所產生的中間代謝物)這種物質少量會與鹼性物質結合而排出體外，過多則會引起體內中毒，甚至危及生命。為預防酮體的產生，並保持充沛的體力，每日至少要攝取50～100公克的醣類(每碗飯含醣約60公克參考第120頁食物代換表)；即使要減肥，也不能僅以多量的蔬果代替醣類，每日至少仍須攝取二碗飯，才不會影響健康。

3.幫助您容易入眠

為什麼飽食後容易愛睏？這是因為醣類會使一種氨基酸容易進入腦中，而這氨基酸是主掌睡眠及行動的一種神經傳遞物，缺乏這種物質，便容易失眠，造成情緒激動。所以，建議失眠的讀者，不妨睡前攝取一點含醣的食物(牛奶、甜點)，可以幫助您進入夢鄉，使器官組織得以休息，次晨才能容光煥發，精力旺盛。

Rice, wheat, barley, oats, whole-wheat, corn, etc. are all considered grains. The root stock category includes potatoes, sweet potatoes, taro, water chestnuts, etc.
The major nutrients which grains and root stocks provide are protein, carbohydrates, and calories. Among these, carbohydrates account for the highest volume of nutrients.

1. THE IMPORTANCE OF PRESERVING THE SOURCE OF MENTAL ENERGY

The active functioning of the brain depends on a constant supply of glucose to the blood. Continuous and severely low levels of blood sugar, caused by such factors as excessive fasting or hunger, will cause irreversible harm to the brain. Furthermore, the only source of glucose in the body is in the form of glycogen stored in the liver. Because the amount is limited (only 100 g.) and thus insufficient for use by the body, it must be absorbed from foods. Grains and rootstocks, which contain a high amount of carbohydrates, supply this need, thereby maintaining the function of the overall central nervous system. So, for those who regularly need to use mental energy for work and school, grains and rootstocks should by all means be included as a part of one's daily diet.

2. PREVENTING EXHAUSTION AND PROMOTING VITALITY

Calories supply the greatest source of physical strength and vitality. Carbohydrates manufacture calories more quickly than do other nutrients, but more calories are supplied by fat. However, if carbohydrates are lacking in the diet, not only are fats unable to oxidize completely and produce calories, but ketones are manufactured excessively as a result. A small amount of this substance will unite with alkaline substances and be expelled from the body. But an excessive amount will result in poisoning of the body and might prove life-threatening. In order to prevent the production of ketones, one must maintain top physical strength. One should consume at least 50-100 g. carbohydrates daily (each bowl of rice contains approx. 60 g. carbohydrates) (Please refer to the exchange table on p. 120) If one is dieting, it is not advisable to merely substitute carbohydrates with a greater amount of vegetables. One should still consume at least two bowls of rice (or eight portions of grains and root stocks) daily so that one's health won't be affected.

3. HELPING YOU FALL ASLEEP EASILY

Why is it that you feel sleepy following a meal? Carbohydrates easily enable one type of amino acid to enter the brain. Furthermore, this amino acid is a type of nerve messenger which controls sleep and activity. If this substance is deficient, insomnia and irritability often result. Thus, it is suggested that readers with insomnia consume a bit of food which contains carbohydrates (milk, dessert) before retiring in the evening. This can help you fall asleep, thereby allowing your organs (and tissues) a rest during the night. Furthermore, in this way you will be able to maintain a radiant disposition during the waking hours.

牛肉粥　BEEF CONGEE

營養含量 Nutritional Content		
蛋白質 Protein	（公克） (g)	16
脂　肪 Fat	（公克） (g)	13
醣 Carbohydrates	（公克） (g)	62
膽固醇 Cholesterol	（毫克） (mg)	34
熱　量 Calories	（大卡） (Cal)	429

1 人份　Per Serving

煮好的稀飯………… 8 碗
牛里肌肉（去筋）‥150 公克
　　　　　　　（ 4 兩）
①{ 醬油………………… 1 小匙
　 酒………………… ½ 小匙
　 太白粉…………… 1 小匙
②{ 鹽………………… 2 小匙
　 胡椒……………… ⅛ 小匙
　 味精……………… ½ 小匙
③{ 嫩薑絲…………… 2 大匙
　 葱絲……………… 2 大匙
　 香菜……………… 4 大匙
番茄或炒熟青菜‥200 公克
　　　　　　（約 5 ½ 兩）

8 bowls congee
(cooked)
1/3 lb. (150 g.) beef loin
(remove tendons)
①{ 1 t. soy sauce
　 1/2 t. cooking wine
　 1 t. cornstarch
②{ 2 t. salt
　 1/8 t. pepper
③{ 2 T. shredded ginger
　　 root
　 2 T. shredded green
　　 onion
　 4 T. coriander
7 oz. (200 g.) tomatoes
or stir-fried green
vegetable

❶牛里肌肉橫紋切薄片，加①料醃 10 分鐘。

❷稀飯加②料調味煮滾，將牛肉加入攪散開至肉片變色（約 30 秒）即熄火，倒入大碗中，撒上③料趁熱食用。

■稀飯煮法：水 16 杯煮開，加米 2 杯（ 320 公克）以大火煮滾，改小火煮至熟爛即可。

❶ Cut beef loin against the grain into thin slices. Add ① and marinate for 10 minutes.

❷ Bring cooked congee and ② to a boil. Add beef and stir to separate. Cook until color changes (for about 30 seconds) and remove from heat. Pour into bowl and sprinkle with ③. Serve hot.

■ To cook congee: Boil 2c. (320 g.) uncooked rice in 16 c. water. Bring 16c. water to a boil. Add 2c. (320 g.) uncooked rice. Bring to a boil over high heat. Reduce heat and simmer until fragant. Serve.

鷄絲泡飯　CHICKEN STRIPS OVER RICE

4 人份　Serves 4

營養含量 Nutritional Content		
蛋白質 Protein	（公克）(g)	17
脂 肪 Fat	（公克）(g)	10
醣 Carbohydrates	（公克）(g)	69
膽固醇 Cholesterol	（毫克）(mg)	31
熱 量 Calories	（大卡）(Cal)	434

1 人份　Per Serving

熟雞肉‥120 公克（約 3 兩）

① 紅蘿蔔…………… 120 公克
筍………………… 120 公克
香菇…………………… 5 朵

高湯…………………… 8 杯

② 醬油………………… 2 大匙
糖…………………… 2 小匙
鹽…………………… 1 小匙
雞油………………… 1 大匙

③ 太白粉……………… 2 大匙
水…………………… 2 大匙

白飯…………………… 4 杯

④ 黑醋………………… 2 小匙
胡椒……………… ¼ 小匙
麻油………………… 1 小匙

香菜………………… 2 大匙

1/4 lb. (120 g.) chicken meat (cooked)

① 1/4 lb. (120 g.) carrots
1/4 lb. (120 g.) bamboo shoots
5 Chinese black mushrooms (soaked)

8 c. broth

② 2 T. soy sauce
2 t. sugar
1 t. salt
1 T. chicken fat

③ 2 T. each: cornstarch, water (mixed)

4 c. cooked rice

④ 2 t. black vinegar
1/4 t. pepper
1 t. sesame oil

2 T. coriander

❶雞肉撕成絲，①料切絲備用。

❷高湯煮開，入①料煮熟，加②料及雞絲待滾，以③料勾芡，淋在飯上，並加④料，上置少許香菜即可。

❶ Tear chicken into strips. Cut ① into strips and set aside.

❷ Bring broth to a boil. Add ① and cook until done. Add ② and chicken strips. Bring to a boil. Thicken with ③. Pour over rice. Season with ④. When serving, garnish with coriander.

荷葉包
TAIWANESE STEAMED TURNOVERS

4 人份　Serves 4

營養含量 Nutritional Content		
蛋白質 Protein	（公克） (g)	16
脂　肪 Fat	（公克） (g)	14
醣 Carbohydrates	（公克） (g)	65
膽固醇 Cholesterol	（毫克） (mg)	25
熱　量 Calories	（大卡） (Cal)	450

1 人份　Per Serving

荷葉包（大）………… 4 個
酸菜‥200 公克（約 5 ½ 兩）
叉燒肉‥120 公克（約 3 兩）
薑絲……………… 1 大匙
①{ 糖……………… 2 小匙
　 味精……………… ⅛ 小匙
花生粉………… 1 大匙
香菜……………… 2 大匙
沙拉油…………… 2 大匙

4 large steamed
　turnovers
7 oz. (200 g.) pickled
　mustard cabbage
4 oz. (120 g.)
　barbecued pork
1 T. ginger root (strips)
2 t. sugar
1 T. peanut powder
2 T. coriander
2 T. vegetable oil

❶酸菜切絲，叉燒肉（做法參考第 19 頁）切片。

❷油 2 大匙燒熱，薑絲爆香，入酸菜及①料炒勻取出。

❸取荷葉包，包入酸菜、肉片、花生粉及香菜即可。

■酸菜如太酸，可先泡水 30 分鐘後擠乾使用。

■叉燒肉可用雞、鴨、牛肉代替。

■可以香菜、小紅蘿蔔等彩盤。

❶ Cut cabbage into strips. Slice barbecued pork. (Refer to page 19).

❷ Heat 2 T. oil in preheated wok. Stir-fry ginger strips until fragrant. Add cabbage and 2 t. sugar; stir-fry until mixed well. Remove from heat.

❸ Fill steamed turnovers with cabbage, pork slices, peanut powder, and coriander. Serve.

■ If pickled mustard cabbage is too sour, it may be soaked in water for 30 minutes and squeezed dry before using.

■ Chicken, duck, and beef may be substituted for barbecued pork.

■ Coriander and small carrots may be used as garnish.

鮪魚三明治 CHINESE-STYLE TUNA FISH SANDWICH

4 人份　Serves 4

營養含量 Nutritional Content		
蛋白質 Protein	（公克） (g)	15
脂　肪 Fat	（公克） (g)	17
醣 Carbohydrates	（公克） (g)	56
膽固醇 Cholesterol	（毫克） (mg)	20
熱　量 Calories	（大卡） (Cal)	437

1 人份　Per Serving

鮪魚（罐裝）……… 120 公克
　　　　　　　（約 3 兩）
馬鈴薯………… 200 公克
　　　　　　　（約 5 ½ 兩）
① { 洋葱末…………… 1 小匙
　 沙拉醬…………… 3 大匙
番茄‥100 公克（約 2 ½ 兩）
小黃瓜… 80 公克（約 2 兩）
吐司……………… 12 片
沙拉醬…………… 3 大匙
生菜……………… 4 葉

4-1/4 oz. (120 g.)
　tunafish (canned)
1/2 lb. (200 g.) potatoes
① { 1 t. onion (minced)
　 3 T. mayonnaise
1/4 lb. (100 g.) tomatoes
1/5 lb. (80 g.) gherkin
　cucumbers
12 slices bread
3 T. mayonnaise
4 leaves lettuce

❶鮪魚搗碎，馬鈴薯去皮煮熟搗成泥，一同加入①料拌勻。番茄、小黃瓜切片。

❷將每片吐司分別塗上沙拉醬，每人份三片，夾上鮪魚醬和番茄、小黃瓜及生菜等材料依次做好，並切成喜愛之形狀即可。

■可以巴西利、番茄、櫻桃彩盤。

❶ Mash tuna. Peel potatoes and boil until done. Mash potatoes. Mix tuna and potato with ① . Slice tomato and gherkin cucumber.

❷ Spread mayonnaise on each slice of bread. Divide and spread tuna mixture, tomato, cucumber, and lettuce on 3 slices of bread to make one sandwich. Continue to make other sandwiches. Cut sandwiches into desired shape.

■ Parsley, tomatoes, and cherries may be used as garnish.

咖哩炒飯　CURRY FRIED RICE

營養含量 Nutritional Content		
蛋白質 Protein	（公克）(g)	28
脂 肪 Fat	（公克）(g)	24
醣 Carbohydrates	（公克）(g)	109
膽固醇 Cholesterol	（毫克）(mg)	43
熱 量 Calories	（大卡）(Cal)	764

1 人份　Per Serving

里肌肉⋯⋯⋯⋯⋯ 250 公克
　　　　　　（約 6 ½ 兩）
① ｛醬油⋯⋯⋯⋯⋯⋯⋯ 2 小匙
　　酒⋯⋯⋯⋯⋯⋯⋯⋯ ½ 小匙
　　太白粉⋯⋯⋯⋯⋯⋯ 2 小匙
② ｛洋蔥⋯ 200 公克（約 5 ½ 兩）
　　葱花⋯⋯⋯⋯⋯⋯⋯ 2 大匙
③ ｛鹽⋯⋯⋯⋯⋯⋯⋯⋯ 1 小匙
　　味精⋯⋯⋯⋯⋯⋯⋯ ¼ 小匙
　　咖哩粉⋯⋯⋯⋯⋯⋯ 2 大匙
胚芽米飯⋯⋯⋯⋯⋯⋯ 7 碗
熟豌豆⋯⋯⋯⋯⋯ 100 公克
　　　　　　（約 2 ½ 兩）
沙拉油⋯⋯⋯⋯⋯⋯ 4 大匙

1/2 lb. (250 g.) pork loin
① ｛2 t. soy sauce
　　1/2 t. cooking wine
　　2 t. cornstarch
② ｛1/2 lb. (200 g.) onion
　　2 T. green onion
　　　(chopped)
③ ｛1 t. salt
　　2 T. curry powder
7 bowls germinated
　rice
3-1/2 oz. (100 g.) peas
　(cooked)
4 T. vegetable oil

❶里肌肉切 1 公分四方小丁，加①料拌勻，洋蔥切丁備用。

❷油燒熱，倒入肉丁炒至變色盛起，餘油炒香②料，並加③料略炒隨入飯炒勻，再加肉丁、豌豆拌炒即可。

❶ Cut pork loin into 1/2″ cubes .Add ① and mix. Cut onion into cubes and set aside.

❷ Heat 4 T.oil in preheated wok. Add pork cubes and stir-fry until color changes. Remove from heat. In remaining oil, stir-fry ② until fragrant. Add ③ and rapidly stir-fry. Mix in cooked rice. Mix in pork cubes and peas. Serve.

原鍋滑鷄飯 CHICKEN OVER RICE

營養含量 Nutritional Content		
蛋白質 Protein	（公克） (g)	26
脂 肪 Fat	（公克） (g)	25
醣 Carbohydrates	（公克） (g)	110
膽固醇 Cholesterol	（毫克） (mg)	55
熱 量 Calories	（大卡） (Cal)	769

1 人份　Per Serving

雞腿⋯⋯⋯ 300 公克（ 8 兩）

① 薑酒汁⋯⋯⋯⋯⋯⋯ 1 大匙
　　醬油⋯⋯⋯⋯⋯⋯⋯ 3 大匙
　　鹽⋯⋯⋯⋯⋯⋯⋯ ½ 小匙
　　糖⋯⋯⋯⋯⋯⋯⋯⋯ 1 小匙
　　麻油⋯⋯⋯⋯⋯⋯⋯ 2 小匙
　　葱花⋯⋯⋯⋯⋯⋯⋯ 1 大匙

胚芽米 560 公克（約 15 兩）
水⋯⋯⋯⋯⋯⋯⋯⋯⋯ 3¾ 杯

② 筍丁⋯⋯⋯ 150 公克（ 4 兩）
　　紅蘿蔔丁⋯⋯⋯⋯ 150 公克
　　雞油（或熟油）⋯⋯⋯ 4 大匙

2/3 lb. (300 g.) chicken legs

① 1 T. ginger wine
　 3 T. soy sauce
　 1/2 t. salt
　 1 t. sugar
　 2 t. sesame oil
　 1 T. green onion (chopped)

1-1/4 lb. (560 g.) germinated rice
3-3/4 c. water

② 1/3 lb. (150 g.) bamboo shoots (cubed)
　 1/3 lb. (150 g.) carrots (cubed)
　 4 T. chicken fat (or fried oil)

❶雞腿切塊，加①料拌醃 20 分鐘備用。

❷胚芽米加水先泡 20 分鐘，加②料拌勻，以大火煮滾 5 分鐘，再擺上雞塊及調味汁，以小火煮 15 分鐘後，熄火再燜 5 分鐘至飯、肉皆熟即可。

■亦可用電鍋煮熟（水改為 3¼ 杯）

❶ Chop chicken legs into pieces. Add ① and marinate for 20 minutes. Set aside.

❷ Add water to germinated rice and soak for 20 minutes. Add ② and mix evenly. Boil over high heat for 5 minutes. Pour chicken and ① over rice mixture. Simmer over low heat for 15 minutes. Remove from heat and cover: Let stand for 5 minutes until rice and chicken are done.

■ Rice and chicken may also be cooked in an electric rice cooker with 3-1/4c. water; remove and serve.

家常叉燒飯 BARBECUED PORK OVER RICE

營養含量 Nutritional Content		
蛋白質 Protein	（公克） (g)	27
脂　肪 Fat	（公克） (g)	24
醣 Carbohydrates	（公克） (g)	114
膽固醇 Cholesterol	（毫克） (mg)	43
熱　量 Calories	（大卡） (Cal)	780

1 人份　Per Serving

前腿瘦肉‥‥‥‥‥ 250 公克
　　　　　　　（約 6 ½ 兩）
① 醬油‥‥‥‥‥‥‥‥ 1 大匙
　蠔油‥‥‥‥‥‥‥‥ 1 大匙
　糖‥‥‥‥‥‥‥‥ 1 ½ 大匙
　酒‥‥‥‥‥‥‥‥‥ 1 大匙
② 蒜頭‥‥‥‥‥‥‥‥ 3 瓣
　葱(切段)‥‥‥‥‥‥ 3 枝
　水‥‥‥‥‥‥‥‥‥ ½ 杯
　胚芽米飯‥‥‥‥‥‥ 7 碗
　炒熟青菜‥‥‥‥‥ 200 公克
　　　　　　　（約 5 ½ 兩）
　熟紅蘿蔔(切條)‥ 100 公克
　　　　　　　（約 2 ½ 兩）
　沙拉油‥‥‥‥‥‥‥ 4 大匙

1/2 lb. (250 g.) boneless
　　pork leg roast
① 1 T. soy sauce
　1 T. oyster sauce
　1-1/2 T. sugar
　1 T. cooking wine
② 3 cloves garlic
　3 stalks green onion,
　　cut into sections
　1/2 c. water
　7 bowls germinated
　　rice (cooked)
　1/2 lb. (200 g.) green
　　vegetable (stir-fried)
　1/4 lb. (100 g.) carrots
　　(cooked and cut into
　　sticks)
　4 T. vegetable oil

❶前腿肉切成長條狀(約 4 × 4 公分)，加①料醃 1 小時以上使入味。

❷油 4 大匙燒熱，將②料爆香，入醃好的肉條、醃汁等並加水 ½ 杯煮開，改小火煮至汁將收乾即可取出切片。

❸飯盛盤上，排上叉燒肉、青菜、紅蘿蔔即可。

■爲增美觀，①料可加少許食用紅色素。

■可以少許香菜彩盤。

❶ Slice pork into long blocks of 1-1/2″ square width. Add ① and marinate for one hour.

❷ Heat 4 T. oil in preheated wok. Add ② and stir-fry quickly until fragrant. Add marinated pork and remaining marinade. Add 1/2 c. water and bring to a boil. Reduce heat and simmer until liquid is almost absorbed. Remove from heat and slice.

❸ Place rice on serving plate. Arrange pork, green vegetable, and carrots over rice.

■ A small amount of red coloring may be added to ① for color enhancement.

■ Coriander may be used as garnish.

鳳梨飯　PINEAPPLE RICE

營養含量 Nutritional Content		
蛋白質 Protein	（公克） (g)	28
脂　肪 Fat	（公克） (g)	24
醣 Carbohydrates	（公克） (g)	114
膽固醇 Cholesterol	（毫克） (mg)	45
熱　量 Calories	（大卡） (Cal)	784

1 人份　Per Serving

鳳梨　200 公克(約 5 ½ 兩)

① ┌ 香腸⋯⋯⋯ 150 公克(4 兩)
　│ 青豆仁⋯⋯⋯⋯⋯ 100 公克
　│ 　　　　　　　（約 2 ½ 兩）
　└ 紅蘿蔔丁⋯⋯⋯⋯ 100 公克

② ┌ 葱花⋯⋯⋯⋯⋯⋯ 1 大匙
　└ 蒜末⋯⋯⋯⋯⋯⋯ 1 小匙

③ ┌ 鹽⋯⋯⋯⋯⋯⋯⋯ 1 小匙
　│ 味精⋯⋯⋯⋯⋯⋯ ¼ 小匙
　└ 胡椒⋯⋯⋯⋯⋯⋯ ¼ 小匙

胚芽米飯⋯⋯⋯⋯⋯⋯ 7 碗
肉鬆⋯⋯ 30 公克(約 1 兩)
沙拉油⋯⋯⋯⋯⋯⋯ 4 大匙

1/2 lb. (200 g.)
　pineapple

① ┌ 1/3 lb. (150 g.) sausage
　│ 　(or ham)
　│ 1/4 lb. (100 g.) green
　│ 　peas
　└ 1/4 lb. (100 g.) carrots
　　 (diced)

② ┌ 1 T. green onions
　│ 　(chopped)
　└ 1 t. garlic cloves
　　 (minced)

③ ┌ 1 t. salt
　└ 1/4 t. black pepper

7 bowls germinated
　rice (cooked)
1 oz. (30 g.) fried
　shredded pork
4 T. vegetable oil

❶鳳梨切小塊，香腸以溫油小火炸熟，取出切片。青豆仁、紅蘿蔔燙熟備用。

❷油 4 大匙燒熱，將②料爆香，下鳳梨及①料炒數下，隨入③料及飯炒勻，盛於盤上，撒上肉鬆即可。

■宴客時，可用鳳梨盅盛飯，以增美觀。

❶ Cut pineapple into small pieces. Heat oil to warm in preheated wok. Fry Chinese sausage over low heat until done. Remove from heat and slice. Boil green peas and carrots until done. Set aside.

❷ Heat 4 T. oil in preheated wok. Quickly stir-fry ② until fragrant. Add pineapple and ①. Stir-fry quickly. Add ③ and rice; stir to mix. Remove from heat and arrange on serving plate. Sprinkle with shredded pork . Serve.

■ When entertaining, rice may be served in hollow pineapple shell.

糖醋排骨飯
SWEET AND SOUR SPARERIBS WITH RICE

營養含量 Nutritional Content		
蛋白質 Protein	（公克）(g)	25
脂　肪 Fat	（公克）(g)	26
醣 Carbohydrates	（公克）(g)	113
膽固醇 Cholesterol	（毫克）(mg)	45
熱　量 Calories	（大卡）(Cal)	786

1 人份　Per Serving

小排骨…………… 350 公克
　　　　　　（約 9 ½ 兩）
① 醬油………………… 2 小匙
　 酒…………………… 1 小匙
　 麵粉………………… 3 大匙
② 青椒… 50 公克（約 1 ½ 兩）
　 熟紅蘿蔔……… 100 公克
　　　　　　（約 2 ½ 兩）
　 青江菜………… 200 公克
　　　　　　（約 5 ½ 兩）
　 蒜末……………… 1 小匙
③ 糖、醋……… 各 6 大匙
　 番茄醬…………… 6 大匙
　 鹽……………… ¼ 小匙
　 水………………… 6 大匙
　 太白粉…………… 1 小匙
胚芽米飯…………… 5 碗
沙拉油……………… 3 杯

3/4 lb. (350 g.) spareribs
① { 2 t. soy sauce
    1 t. cooking wine
    3 T. flour
② { 1-3/4 oz. (50 g.) green
      pepper
    1/4 lb. (100 g.) carrots
      (cooked)
    1/2 lb. (200 g.) bok choy
    1 t. garlic clove
      (minced)
③ { 6 T. each: sugar,
      vinegar, ketchup
    1/4 t. salt
    6 T. water
    1 t. cornstarch
5 bowls germinated
  rice (cooked)
3 c. vegetable oil

❶小排骨切 3 公分方塊，加①料醃 20 分鐘，炸前裹上麵粉。

❷青椒、紅蘿蔔切塊，青江菜煮熟備用。

❸油燒熱，入肉塊炸熟（約 3 分鐘）並呈金黃色撈出，留油 1 大匙，炒香蒜末，入②料炒數下，隨入③料煮開，再下肉塊拌勻即成。

❹飯盛盤上，擺上做好之糖醋排骨及青菜即可。

❶ Slice spareribs into 1-1/4″ squares . Add ① and marinate for 20 minutes. Coat in flour before frying.

❷ Cut green pepper and carrots into pieces. Boil bok choy until done.

❸ Heat 3 c. oil in preheated wok. Add sparerib squares and deep-fry until golden (approx. 3 minutes). Remove squares with strainer. Leave 1 T. oil in wok. Stir-fry minced garlic until fragrant. Add ② and quickly stir-fry. Add ③ and bring to a boil. Add sparerib squares; stir until mixed well.

❹ Arrange cooked rice on serving plate. Add sweet and sour pork and green vegetable to side. Serve.

砂鍋菜飯　SIMMERED SHRIMP-FRIED RICE

營養含量 Nutritional Content		
蛋白質 Protein	（公克） (g)	29
脂　肪 Fat	（公克） (g)	25
醣 Carbohydrates	（公克） (g)	108
膽固醇 Cholesterol	（毫克） (mg)	87
熱　量 Calories	（大卡） (Cal)	773

1 人份　Per Serving

中式火腿⋯⋯⋯⋯ 90 公克
　　　　　（約 2 ½ 兩）
蝦仁⋯⋯ 180 公克（約 5 兩）
① { 酒⋯⋯⋯⋯⋯⋯⋯⋯ 1 小匙
　　 鹽⋯⋯⋯⋯⋯⋯⋯⋯ ¼ 小匙
　　 太白粉⋯⋯⋯⋯⋯⋯ 1 小匙
青江菜⋯⋯ 300 公克（8 兩）
葱花⋯⋯⋯⋯⋯⋯⋯⋯ 2 大匙
② { 鹽⋯⋯⋯⋯⋯⋯⋯⋯ ½ 小匙
　　 味精⋯⋯⋯⋯⋯⋯⋯ ¼ 小匙
　　 水⋯⋯⋯⋯⋯⋯⋯⋯ 1 大匙
胚芽米飯⋯⋯⋯⋯⋯⋯ 7 碗
沙拉油⋯⋯⋯⋯⋯⋯⋯ 4 大匙

3 oz. (90 g.) Chinese-style ham
6 oz. (180 g.) shrimp (shelled)
① { 1 t. cooking wine
　　 1/4 t. salt
　　 1 t. cornstarch
2/3 lb. (300 g.) bok choy
2 T. green onion (chopped)
② { 1/2 t. salt
　　 1 T. water
7 bowls germinated rice
4 T. vegetable oil

❶火腿蒸熟（約 20 分鐘），取出切 2 公分正方薄片，蝦仁加①料醃 10 分鐘，青江菜切 2 公分長段備用。

❷油燒熱，入葱花爆香，下蝦仁炒至變色，隨入火腿、青江菜炒數下，再入②料及飯炒勻，以小火燜 5 分鐘即可。

■中式火腿可以洋火腿（免蒸）替代

❶ Steam ham until done (approximately 20 minutes). Remove and thinly slice into 3/4" square pieces. Add ① to shrimp and marinate for 10 minutes. Slice bok choy into sections, 3/4" long. Set aside.

❷ Heat 4 T. oil in preheated wok. Add chopped green onion and stir-fry until fragrant. Add shrimp and stir-fry until color changes. Add ham and bok choy; stir-fry to mix. Add ② and cooked rice. Mix well and simmer over low heat for 5 minutes. Serve.

■ Western-style ham (steaming not necessary) may be substituted for Chinese-style ham.

五彩涼麵　COLD RAINBOW NOODLES

營養含量 Nutritional Content		
蛋白質 Protein	（公克）(g)	27
脂 肪 Fat	（公克）(g)	26
醣 Carbohydrates	（公克）(g)	109
膽固醇 Cholesterol	（毫克）(mg)	158
熱 量 Calories	（大卡）(Cal)	778

1 人份　Per Serving

① ⎰ 麵條… 520 公克（約 14 兩）
　　沙拉油……………… 2 大匙

　⎧ 小黃瓜…… 150 公克（4 兩）
　⎪ 紅蘿蔔………… 150 公克
① ⎨ 叉燒肉………… 150 公克
　⎪ 蛋……………………… 2 個

　⎧ 芝麻醬………… 4 大匙
　⎪ 醬油……………… 4 大匙
　⎪ 糖………………… 2 大匙
　⎪ 檸檬汁…………… 3 大匙
② ⎨ 蒜泥……………… 1 大匙
　⎪ 麻油……………… ½ 大匙
　⎪ 薑汁……………… 2 大匙
　⎩ 冷開水…………… 6 大匙

1-1/4 lb. (520 g.) noodles
2 T. vegetable oil

① ⎧ 1/3 lb. (150 g.) gherkin
　⎪ 　cucumbers
　⎨ 1/3 lb. (150 g.) carrots
　⎪ 1/3 lb. (150 g.)
　⎪ 　barbecued pork
　⎩ 2 eggs

② ⎧ 4 T. sesame paste (or
　⎪ 　peanut butter)
　⎪ 4 T. soy sauce
　⎪ 2 T. sugar
　⎨ 3 T. lemon juice
　⎪ 1 T. garlic paste
　⎪ 1/2 T. sesame oil
　⎪ 2 T. ginger juice
　⎩ 6 T. cold water

❶麵條入滾水中煮熟（約 5 ～ 7 分鐘），取出沖冷開水後拌入沙拉油 2 大匙置盤上，蛋打散煎成蛋皮，②料拌勻備用

❷①料切絲，排於麵上，食時淋上②料並拌勻即可。

❶ Place noodles in boiling water and cook until done (about 5-7 minutes). Remove and rinse in cold water. Mix with 2 T. vegetable oil in bowl. Beat eggs and fry to make thin omelet. Mix ②.

❷ Slice ① into strips and arrange on noodles. When ready to serve, pour ② over noodles. Mix well and serve.

茄汁拌麵 NOODLES IN TOMATO SAUCE

營養含量 Nutritional Content		
蛋白質 Protein	（公克） (g)	26
脂　肪 Fat	（公克） (g)	24
醣 Carbohydrates	（公克） (g)	111
膽固醇 Cholesterol	（毫克） (mg)	58
熱　量 Calories	（大卡） (Cal)	764

1 人份　Per Serving

麵條(乾)·········· 520 公克
　　　　　　　（約 14 兩）
沙拉油·············· 1 大匙
洋葱········ 75 公克（2 兩）
① 芹菜·············· 75 公克
　洋菇(切片)······· 100 公克
　　　　　　　（約 2½ 兩）
　豌豆仁 50 公克（約 1½ 兩）
牛絞肉············ 250 公克
　　（或豬絞肉，約 6½ 兩）
② 水····· 1 杯，糖····· 2 小匙
　番茄醬············ 6 大匙
　鹽··············· ½ 小匙
　酒··············· 1 小匙
③ 太白粉·········· 1½ 小匙
　水··············· 1 大匙
沙拉油·············· 3 大匙

1-1/4 oz. (520 g.)
　　noodles (dry)
1 T. vegetable oil
2-2/3 oz. (75 g.) onion
① 2-2/3 oz. (75 g.) celery
　3-1/2 oz. (100 g.) button
　　mushrooms (sliced)
　1-3/4 oz. (50 g.) green
　　peas
1/2 lb. (250 g.) ground
　beef (or ground pork)
② 1 c. water
　6 T. ketchup
　2 t. sugar
　1/2 t. salt
　1 t. cooking wine
③ 1-1/2 t. cornstarch } mix
　1 T. water
3 T. vegetable oil

❶水煮開，下麵條煮熟，撈起後加 1 大匙油拌勻置盤上，洋葱、芹菜切碎，洋菇、豌豆仁燙熟備用。

❷油 3 大匙燒熱，洋葱末炒香，入絞肉炒鬆，加入②料待滾，以③ 料勾芡，隨入①料拌勻，淋在煮好的麵上，食時拌勻即可。

❶ Bring water to a boil. Add noodles and cook until done. Remove and drain. Add 1 T. oil to noodles, mix evenly, and arrange on serving plate. Mince onions and celery. Boil mushrooms and peas until done and set aside.

❷ Heat 3 T. oil in preheated wok. Stir-fry minced onions until fragrant. Add ground beef and stir-fry until meat separates. Add ② and bring to a boil. Thicken with ③. Add ① and stir to mix. Pour over cooked noodles. Mix together when ready to serve.

通心麵沙拉 CHINESE—STYLE MACARONI SALAD

營養含量 Nutritional Content		
蛋白質 Protein	（公克） (g)	28
脂 肪 Fat	（公克） (g)	24
醣 Carbohydrates	（公克） (g)	110
膽固醇 Cholesterol	（毫克） (mg)	63
熱 量 Calories	（大卡） (Cal)	768

1 人份　Per Serving

① 通心麵(乾)⋯⋯⋯ 560 公克
　　　　　　　　（約 15 兩）
　洋火腿 60 公克(約 1 ½ 兩)
　熟蝦仁⋯⋯⋯⋯⋯ 60 公克
　熟雞肉 90 公克(約 2 ½ 兩)
　熟紅蘿蔔⋯⋯⋯⋯ 100 公克
　　　　　　　　（約 2 ½ 兩）
　小黃瓜⋯150 公克(約 4 兩)
　芹菜⋯ 50 公克(約 1 ½ 兩)

② 沙拉醬⋯⋯⋯⋯⋯⋯ ½ 杯
　鹽⋯⋯⋯⋯⋯⋯⋯ ¼ 小匙
　糖⋯⋯⋯⋯⋯⋯⋯ 1 小匙
　胡椒粉⋯⋯⋯⋯⋯ ¼ 小匙

① 1-1/4 lb. (560 g.)
　　macaroni (dry)
　2 oz. (60 g.) Western-
　　style ham
　2 oz. (60 g.) shrimp
　　(shelled and cooked)
　3 oz. (90 g.) chicken
　　meat (cooked)
　3-1/2 oz. (100 g.) carrots
　　(cooked)
　1/3 lb. (150 g.) gherkin
　　cucumbers
　1-3/4 oz. (50 g.) celery

② 1/2 c. mayonnaise
　1/4 t. salt
　1 t. sugar
　1/4 t. pepper

❶水煮開，下通心麵煮熟(約 10 分鐘)撈出。洋火腿、雞肉、紅蘿蔔、小黃瓜皆切丁(1 公分正方)，芹菜切末。

❷將①料全部置盆中，加②料拌勻盛盤上即可。

❶ Bring water to a boil. Add macaroni and cook until done (approximately 10 minutes). Remove with slotted spoon. Cut ham, chicken, carrots, and gherkin cucumbers into 1/2" cubes. Mince celery.

❷ Place ① in bowl. Add ② and mix well, arrange on plate and serve.

麵片湯　NOODLE SLICE SOUP

4 人份　Serves 4

營養含量 Nutritional Content		
蛋白質 Protein	（公克）(g)	30
脂　肪 Fat	（公克）(g)	25
醣 Carbohydrates	（公克）(g)	117
膽固醇 Cholesterol	（毫克）(mg)	50
熱　量 Calories	（大卡）(Cal)	813

1 人份　Per Serving

① { 麵粉····················· 5 杯
　　 水······················· 1 ¾ 杯
　　 瘦肉········ 300 公克（ 8 兩）
② { 酒、醬油·········· 各 1 小匙
　　 太白粉··············· 1 大匙
③ { 香菇(泡軟)··········· 4 朵
　　 草菇··100 公克(約 2 ½ 兩)
　　 紅蘿蔔··········· 100 公克
　　 熟筍··200 公克(約 5 ½ 兩)
　　 蔥(3 公分長)········· 3 段
　　 水(或高湯)·········· 10 杯
④ { 鹽··················· 2 ½ 小匙
　　 味精·············· ½ 小匙
　　 醬油················· 2 大匙
　　 胡椒················· ¼ 小匙
　　 麻油·············· ½ 小匙
　　 沙拉油·············· 4 大匙

① { 5 c. flour
　　 1-3/4 c. water
　　 2/3 lb. (300 g.) pork loin
② { 1 t. each: cooking
　　　 wine, soy sauce
　　 1 T. cornstarch
③ { 4 Chinese black
　　　 mushrooms (soaked
　　　 until soft)
　　 1/4 lb. (100 g.) each:
　　　 straw mushrooms,
　　　 carrots
　　 1/2 lb. (200 g.) bamboo
　　　 shoots (cooked)
　　 3 sections green onion
　　　 (1-1/4")
　　 10 c. water (or broth)
④ { 2-1/2 t. salt
　　 2 T. soy sauce
　　 1/4 t. pepper
　　 1/2 t. sesame oil
　　 4 T. vegetable oil

❶將①料和成麵糰，搓成長條狀（直徑約 3 公分），入冷水中泡約 20 分鐘，以增加延展性。

❷瘦肉切(0.2×3×4 公分)薄片，加②料醃 10 分鐘，筍、紅蘿蔔切片狀。

❸油 4 大匙燒熱，將肉片炒至變色取出，餘油將蔥段爆香，加水煮開，隨入③料煮滾，取出水中之麵糰，以手拉成薄片，投入滾湯中煮熟，隨入炒好的肉片及④料調味即可。

■可以香菜點綴。

❶ Mix ① to make dough. Knead into long cylinder (approx. 1-1/4" diameter). Soak in cold water for 20 minutes to increase elasticity.

❷ Cut pork into thin slices, 1-1/2" x 1-1/4". Add ② and marinate for 10 minutes. Slice bamboo shoots and carrots.

❸ Heat 4 T. oil in preheated wok. Add pork slices and stir-fry until color changes. Remove pork from heat. In remaining oil, stir-fry green onion sections until fragrant. Add water and bring to a boil. Add ③ and bring to another boil. Remove dough from water and pinch into thin slices. Add to boiling soup and cook until done. Add stir-fried pork slices and season with ④. Serve.

■ Coriander may be used as garnish.

水餃

BOILED DUMPLINGS

4 人份　Serves 4

營養含量 Nutritional Content		
蛋白質 Protein	（公克）(g)	29
脂 肪 Fat	（公克）(g)	23
醣 Carbohydrates	（公克）(g)	111
膽固醇 Cholesterol	（毫克）(mg)	68
熱 量 Calories	（大卡）(Cal)	767

1 人份　Per Serving

牛絞肉‥‥‥ 300 公克（ 8 兩）

① ┌ 大白菜‥‥‥‥‥‥ 300 公克
　│ 韭黃‥100 公克(約 2 ½ 兩)
　│ 紅蘿蔔‥‥‥‥‥‥ 100 公克
　│ 粉絲‥‥ 60 公克(約 1 ½ 兩)
　└ 鹽‥‥‥‥‥‥‥‥‥ ½ 小匙

② ┌ 水‥‥‥‥‥‥‥‥‥ 2 大匙
　│ 葱、薑末‥‥‥‥‥ 各 2 大匙
　│ 麻油‥‥‥‥‥‥‥ 3 ½ 大匙
　│ 醬油‥‥‥‥‥‥‥‥ 1 大匙
　└ 鹽‥‥‥‥‥‥‥‥‥ ½ 小匙

水餃皮 750 公克（約 75 張）

2/3 lb. (300 g.) ground beef

① ┌ 2/3 lb. (300 g.) Chinese Nappa cabbage
　│ 1/4 lb. (100 g.) yellow Chinese chives
　│ 1/4 lb. (100 g.) carrots
　│ 2 oz. (60 g.) dried bean threads
　└ 1/2 t. salt

② ┌ 2 T. water
　│ 2 T. green onion (minced)
　│ 2 T. ginger root (minced)
　│ 3-1/2 T. sesame oil
　│ 1 T. soy sauce
　└ 1/2 t. salt

1-2/3 lb. (750 g.) dumpling skins/ wrappers (about 75)

❶大白菜切碎加鹽 ½ 小匙醃 5 分鐘後，擠乾水分，韭黃、紅蘿蔔切碎，粉絲泡軟切碎備用。

❷絞肉加②料順同一方向拌至有黏性，約 3 分鐘，再加入①料拌勻成餡。

❸取餃皮，包入餡一份捏緊，依次做好，入滾水中大火煮開，再加 $\frac{2}{3}$ 杯冷水煮滾，最後再加一次冷水煮滾即可撈出，可隨自己喜好沾佐料食之。

■可以香菜、紅蘿蔔彩盤。

❶ Finely chop cabbage. Add 1/2 t. salt and marinate for 5 minutes. Squeeze out excess water. Finely chop chives and carrots. Soak bean threads in water until soft; finely chop and set aside.

❷ Add ② to ground beef. Mix by stirring in one direction until sticky (about 3 minutes). Add ①. Mix evenly to make filling.

❸ Place 1 spoonful of filling in 1 dumpling wrapper. Tightly seal. Repeat until all dumplings have been filled and sealed. Add dumplings to boiling water and bring to a boil over high heat. Add 2/3 c. cold water and bring to another boil. Add another 2/3 c. cold water and bring to a third boil. Remove from heat with slotted spoon. May prepare dip to taste from a combination of soy sauce, vinegar, sesame oil, red chili sauce, chopped green onion, and minced garlic.

■ Coriander and carrots may be used as garnish.

肉粳米粉
PORK AND FISH PASTE OVER RICE NOODLES

4 人份　Serves 4

營養含量 Nutritional Content		
蛋白質 Protein	（公克）(g)	29
脂肪 Fat	（公克）(g)	28
醣 Carbohydrates	（公克）(g)	108
膽固醇 Cholesterol	（毫克）(mg)	44
熱量 Calories	（大卡）(Cal)	800

1 人份　Per Serving

① 瘦肉····· 180 公克（約 5 兩）
　魚漿····· 120 公克（約 3 兩）
　炸香紅蔥頭········· 1 大匙
　米粉······· 600 公克（1 斤）
　香菇絲················· ¼ 杯
② 水················· 12 杯
　鹽、糖、醬油····· 各 2 小匙
③ 金針菇（或筍絲）·· 200 公克
　紅蘿蔔絲········· 100 公克
　柴魚······· 5 公克（約½ 兩）
④ 胡椒················· ¼ 小匙
　麻油················· 1 小匙
　黑醋、沙茶醬····· 各 1 大匙
　香菜················· 2 大匙
　沙拉油················· 4 大匙

① 1/3 lb. (180 g.) pork loin
　4-1/2 oz. (120 g.) fish paste
　1 T. fried shallot slices
　1-1/3 lb. (600 g.) rice noodles
　1/4 c. Chinese black mushrooms (soaked and cut into strips)
② 12 c. water
　2 t. each: salt, sugar, soy sauce
③ 1/2 lb. (200 g.) golden mushrooms (or bamboo shoots)
　1/4 lb. (100 g.) carrots (strips)
　1/6 oz. (5 g.) dried benito shavings
④ 1 T. black vinegar
　1/4 t. pepper
　1 t. sesame oil
　1 T. Chinese barbecue sauce
　2 T. coriander
　4 T. vegetable oil

❶瘦肉切 2×5 公分長薄片，加醬油 1 小匙、太白粉 2 小匙稍拌，再與①料攪勻，米粉以冷水泡軟（約 15 分鐘）。

❷油 4 大匙燒熱，下香菇炒香，入②料及③料煮滾，投入肉片待滾，隨即以太白粉、水各 6 大匙勾芡即為肉粳。

❸米粉以滾水煮熟置湯碗中，淋上肉粳，並加④料及香菜即可。

■如無柴魚可免用。

❶ Cut pork into thin slices, 2″ x 3/4″. Mix 1t. soy sauce with 2t. cornstarch and blend in ①. Soak rice noodles in water until soft (about 15 minutes).

❷ Heat 4 T. oil in preheated wok. Add mushrooms and stir-fry until fragrant. Add ② and ③. Bring to a boil. Add meat slices and bring to another boil. Thicken with cornstarch and water mixture (6T. each).

❸ Cook noodles in boiling water until done. Remove with slotted spoon and place in soup bowl. Pour pork over noodles. Season with ④ and garnish with coriander.

■ Dried benito shavings may be omitted from recipe if unavailable.

肉燥河粉
MEAT SAUCE OVER BROAD RICE NOODLES

4 人份　Serves 4

營養含量 Nutritional Content		
蛋白質 Protein	（公克） (g)	27
脂　肪 Fat	（公克） (g)	25
醣 Carbohydrates	（公克） (g)	110
膽固醇 Cholesterol	（毫克） (mg)	43
熱　量 Calories	（大卡） (Cal)	773

1 人份　Per Serving

紅葱頭(切片)………… 5 瓣
香菇末…………… 1 大匙
絞肉‥250 公克(約 6 ½ 兩)
① ┌ 酒……………… 1 大匙
　│ 糖…………… 1 ½ 小匙
　│ 醬油………… 4 大匙
　│ 麻油………… 1 小匙
　└ 水……………… 1 杯
② ┌ 河粉(切條)…… 1400 公克
　│ 　　　　(約 2 斤 5 兩)
　│ 綠豆芽………… 200 公克
　│ 　　　　(約 5 ½ 兩)
　│ 紅蘿蔔絲……… 50 公克
　│ 　　　　(約 1 ½ 兩)
　└ 韭菜(切段)……… 50 公克
沙拉油…………… 4 大匙

5 cloves shallots, sliced
1 T. mushroom (minced)
1/2 lb. (250 g.) ground
　pork
① ┌ 1 T. cooking wine
　│ 1-1/2 t. sugar
　│ 4 T. soy sauce
　│ 1 t. sesame oil
　└ 1 c. water
② ┌ 11 lb. (1400 g.) broad
　│ 　rice noodles (strips)
　│ 1/2 lb. (200 g.) mung
　│ 　bean sprouts
　│ 3/4 oz. (50 g.) carrots
　│ 　(strips)
　│ 1-3/4 oz. (50 g.) Chinese
　└ 　chives (strips)
4 T. vegetable oil

❶油 4 大匙燒熱，將紅葱頭以小火炸香，入香菇末、絞肉炒至變色，再加①料煮滾 20 分鐘，即成肉燥。

❷將②料以滾水快速燙熟置盤上，淋上肉燥即可。

❶ Heat 4 T. oil in preheated wok. Deep-fry shallots over low heat until fragrant. Add minced mushroom and ground pork; stir-fry until pork changes color. Add ① and bring to a boil. Reduce heat and simmer for 20 minutes until pork attains meat sauce consistency.

❷ Blanch ② in boiling water until done. Arrange on serving plate. Pour meat sauce over noodles and serve.

肉類

1.常保青春與抵抗疾病的祕訣

肉類含有豐富的蛋白質，而人體的組成除了水外，以蛋白質含量最多。蛋白質不僅是身體的基本建材，舉凡幫助消化吸收與調節生理作用的酵素、賀爾蒙、維持神經傳遞正常的物質，抵抗傳染病的抗體等，都需仰賴蛋白質。

蛋白質由22種氨基酸構成，而其中8種必須從食物中攝取，這8種氨基酸稱爲主要氨基酸，凡蛋白質中有很豐富的8種主要氨基酸，即稱爲完全蛋白質。食物中只有動物性蛋白質含有完全蛋白質；植物蛋白質中，只有黃豆及其製品（如豆腐等）差可比擬。

人在生存的每一瞬間，體內的蛋白質都在細胞內被酵素分解。氨基酸必須源源不斷地供給細胞的需要，而身體各部分也能吸收運用充分的營養時，人才可長保健康青春；相反的，營養不足時，身體就會將比較不重要的組織破壞（如肌肉），取得氨基酸來供應身體組織所需的養分。久而久之，身體或許仍能勉強支持，但血裡的蛋白質、酵素、賀爾蒙及抗體都逐漸減少，不僅使肌肉鬆弛、皺紋出現，有未老先衰之態，甚至體質變弱，易感染疾病。

因此，適當的攝取含有完全蛋白質的食物是很重要的。素食者宜攝取穀類、黃豆及其製品（圖1）、堅果類（圖2）、蕈類（圖3）以補充所需。

2.口齒留香的動物脂肪無須拋棄

動物脂肪中質地最好的是魚貝類及家禽，而家畜類以豬油所含的主要脂肪酸[註]爲多。動物性脂肪具有揮發性的香味，添加少許肉類於蔬菜中，不僅能增加風味，促進食慾，而且能溶解蔬菜中脂溶性維生素，有助人體吸收利用。故而肉類食物中口齒留香的動物性脂肪，只要適當的攝取何須拋棄？

3.消化器官與功能正常的功臣

消化器官正常的蠕動，使食物與消化液及酵素充分混合，再配以健全的酵素及賀爾蒙（二者也是一種蛋白質），才能使食物完全消化吸收。消化過程的每一環都要靠蛋白質，否則消化器官的肌肉韌帶鬆弛無力，酵素及賀爾蒙的製造受阻，大部分食物就會消化不良，而造成便祕或腹瀉。要使消化功能運作正常，蛋白質的供應就要充足，動物性蛋白質就是最佳來源。

4.如何使兒童聰穎機靈

人的智慧及行爲主要受三個因素的影響—遺傳、營養、環境。智慧發展在五歲以前，營養狀況大於環境刺激；尤其是胎兒期到二歲之間，是腦部發育的關鍵期。這個時期，一旦腦部發育不良或受損，則不會恢復，所以尤須注意均衡營養。營養好的兒童不但身體健康、反應靈敏，而且智力較高。

腦發育成熟後，環境刺激固然重要，營養亦不容忽視。使頭腦清醒明澈的醣類，使神經傳遞正常的蛋白質、礦物質及維生素，缺一不可。而其中最能增進腦機能的營養素是蛋白質、鐵質及維生素B羣（見附表第122頁）。總之，均衡飲食之供應，不僅促進兒童健康，亦使兒童聰穎機靈。

[註]：主要脂肪酸是一種不飽和脂肪酸，體內無法自製，必須由食物中獲得。

MEATS

1. MEATS—HELP TO PRESERVE YOUTH AND GUARD AGAINST DISEASE

Meats are rich in protein. Furthermore, the human body, besides being composed of water, also contains a high volume of protein. Protein not only comprises the body's basic make-up but also helps digestion, absorption, and regulation of body processes. Substances which allow for regular nerve transmission as well as antibodies which guard against disease also rely on protein.

Protein is formed from 22 kinds of amino acids among which eight must be provided for in the diet. These eight kinds of amino acids are called essential amino acids. Proteins which are rich in the eight essential acids are called complete proteins. In the diet, only animal proteins contain complete proteins; Among plant proteins, only soybean and its products (such as bean curd) contain a sufficient volume of amino acids.

During every moment of a person's life, the protein in the body is being dissolved by intracellular enzymes. Amino acids must continuously provide cellular needs. Furthermore, only when all parts of the body fully absorb and use nutrients can one regularly preserve one's own health and youth; Conversely, when nutrients are insufficient, the body destroys the less important tissues (such as muscles) and obtains amino acids from them to supply the nutrients needed by the body's other tissues. Over a long period of time, the body **is barely able to support itself. Proteins, enzymes, hormones, and antibodies in the blood** gradually decrease. This not only causes the muscles to slacken, but also results in the appearance of wrinkles, the weakening of one's physical constitution, as well as the contraction of contagious diseases.

Therefore, the proper absorbance of foods which contain complete proteins is essential. Vegetarians tend to consume grains, soybeans (and their products) (illus. 1), nuts (illus. 2), and mushrooms (illus. 3) to supplement such needs.

2. THERE'S NO NEED TO GIVE UP EATING DELICIOUS ANIMAL FATS

The best quality animal fat is that which is found in poultry, fish, and shellfish. Furthermore, the essential fatty acids (see note) contained in pork fat account for the highest among domesticated animals. Animal fat has a succulent aroma which bolsters one's appetite. Also, animal fats are able to dissolve the fat-soluble vitamins contained in vegetables, thereby aiding absorption. As long as a suitable amount is consumed, one need not give up eating tasty animal fats.

3. REGULAR CONTRIBUTOR TO DIGESTIVE ORGANS AND THEIR FUNCTIONS

The regular movement of the digestive organs allows for the complete mixing of food with digestive liquids and enzymes. Food can only be completely absorbed with the aid of healthy enzymes and hormones (which are also a type of protein) in the digestive process. It is thus evident that every part of the digestive process relies on protein. A diet which lacks protein results in the weakening of digestive organ muscles, thereby blocking the production of enzymes and hormones. In this situation, most foods will not be properly absorbed and either diarrhea or constipation will ensue. For the absorption process to function regularly, the supply of protein must be sufficient. Animal protein is its best source.

4. HOW TO ENCOURAGE THE DEVELOPMENT OF INTELLIGENT AND RESPONSIVE CHILDREN

Human intelligence and behavior are primarily influenced by three factors: heredity, nutrition, and environment. Before a child reaches its fifth year, the development of its intellect is influenced more by nutrition than by environmental stimulus. Between the fetal stage and two years of age, if brain development is poor or harmed, recovery is rarely possible. Therefore, balanced nutrition must be especially stressed during this key developmental period. Not only are children who have a nutritious diet healthy, their responses are also quick and their level of intelligence is higher.

When brain development is mature, stimulus from the environment becomes important. Yet nutrition should by no means be neglected. One cannot lack carbohydrates, for they enable the mind to work clearly and intelligently. The body also depends on protein (which enables regular nerve transmission) as well as vitamins and minerals. Among these, those nutrients which are best able to assist the functions of the brain include protein, iron, and Vitamin B complex (see appendix on page 123). Finally, providing children with a balanced diet not only encourages their health but also enables them to develop intelligently and responsively.

Note: Essential fatty acids are a type of unsaturated fatty acid which cannot be manufactured by the body but must be obtained from foods.

吉利鷄柳　BREADED CHICKEN BREAST

營養含量 Nutritional Content		
蛋白質 Protein	（公克）(g)	9
脂　肪 Fat	（公克）(g)	11
醣 Carbohydrates	（公克）(g)	8
膽固醇 Cholesterol	（毫克）(mg)	53
熱　量 Calories	（大卡）(Cal)	167

1 人份　Per Serving

雞胸肉‥‥‥ 150 公克（ 4 兩）

① 　鹽‥‥‥‥‥‥‥ ⅓ 小匙
　糖‥‥‥‥‥‥‥ ½ 小匙
　胡椒‥‥‥‥‥‥ ⅛ 小匙
　酒‥‥‥‥‥‥‥ ½ 小匙
　蒜末‥‥‥‥‥‥ 1 小匙
　太白粉‥‥‥‥‥ 1 大匙
麵粉‥‥‥‥‥‥‥ 2 大匙
蛋‥‥‥‥‥‥‥‥ ½ 個
麵包粉‥‥‥‥‥‥ ½ 杯
沙拉油‥‥‥‥‥‥ 3 杯

1/3 lb. (150 g.) chicken breast

① 　1/3 t. salt
　1/2 t. sugar
　1/8 t. pepper
　1/2 t. cooking wine
　1 t. garlic (minced)
　1 T. cornstarch
2 T. flour
1/2 egg
1/2 c. bread crumbs
3 c. vegetable oil

❶雞胸肉切條狀（ 8 × 1.5 × 1.5 公分），加①料醃 10 分鐘，蛋打成蛋液。

❷雞肉依次裹上麵粉、蛋液、麵包粉，入熱油中炸熟並呈金黃色（約 1 分鐘）即可。

■可以生菜葉彩盤。

❶ Slice chicken into 3"x1/2"x1/2" sticks and marinate in ① for 10 minutes. Beat egg until even.

❷ Dip chicken sticks one at a time into flour, then into egg, and lastly into bread crumbs. Heat 3 c. vegetable oil in preheated wok. Deep-fry chicken for about one minute or until golden brown. Serve.

■ Garnish bottom of serving plate with lettuce.

溜鷄捲　BROCCOLI CHICKEN ROLLS

營養含量 Nutritional Content		
蛋白質 Protein	（公克） (g)	11
脂 肪 Fat	（公克） (g)	11
醣 Carbohydrates	（公克） (g)	1
膽固醇 Cholesterol	（毫克） (mg)	45
熱 量 Calories	（大卡） (Cal)	147

1 人份　Per Serving

雞胸肉 (去骨) 225 公克
　　　　　　　（6 兩 ）

① 鹽·······················⅓ 小匙
酒·······················½ 小匙
蛋白·····················½ 個
太白粉···················1 小匙
芥蘭菜···················12 棵
　　（取梗部 6 公分長）

② 高湯·····················1 杯
鹽·······················⅓ 小匙
胡椒·····················⅛ 小匙
味精·····················¼ 小匙

③ 太白粉···················1 ½ 小匙
水·······················1 大匙
雞油(或熟油)···········1 大匙

1/2 lb. (225 g.) chicken
　breast (boneless)

① 1/3 t. salt
1/2 t. cooking wine
1/2 egg white
1 t. cornstarch
12 stalks Chinese
　broccoli, 2-1/2" long

② 1 c. broth
1/3 t. salt
1/8 t. pepper

③ 1-1/2 t. cornstarch } mix
1 T. water
1 T. chicken fat (or fried
　oil)

❶雞胸肉切長薄片（ 8×3×0.3 公分）共 12 片，以①料醃 10 分鐘。芥蘭菜以滾水燙 30 秒取出。

❷雞肉片捲芥蘭菜排於蒸盤上，水開大火蒸熟(約 3 分鐘)取出排盤上。

❸將②料煮開，以③料勾芡並加雞油 1 大匙，淋於雞捲上即成。

❶ Cut chicken breast into 12 thin slices, (3" x 1-1/4" x 1/8"). Marinate in ① for 10 minutes. Blanch broccoli in boiling water for 30 seconds. Remove broccoli.

❷ Roll each broccoli stalk in one chicken slice and arrange on steaming plate. Steam over high heat until ready (about 3 minutes). Remove from heat.

❸ Boil ②. Thicken with ③ and add 1 T. chicken fat. Pour over chicken rolls and serve.

清蒸滑鷄　STEAMED CHICKEN

營養含量 Nutritional Content		
蛋白質 Protein	（公克） (g)	11
脂　肪 Fat	（公克） (g)	9
醣 Carbohydrates	（公克） (g)	39
膽固醇 Cholesterol	（毫克） (mg)	42
熱　量 Calories	（大卡） (Cal)	137

1 人份　Per Serving

雞腿……… 300 公克(半斤)
香菇………………… 5 朵
葱(3 公分長)……… 2 段
薑………………… 3 片
① 醬油……………… 1 小匙
　鹽……………… 1/3 小匙
　酒……………… 1 小匙
　麻油…………… 1/2 小匙
　太白粉………… 1 小匙
青江菜………… 200 公克
(約 5 1/2 兩)
② 蒸雞汁十高湯(或水)…1 杯
　醬油…………… 1/2 大匙
　麻油…………… 1/2 小匙
③ 太白粉………… 1 1/2 小匙
　水……………… 1 大匙

2/3 lb. (300 g.) chicken legs
5 Chinese black mushrooms
2 stalks green onion (sections)
3 slices ginger root
① 1 t. soy sauce
　1/3 t. salt
　1 t. cooking wine
　1/2 t. sesame oil
　1 t. cornstarch
1/2 lb. (200 g.) bok choy
② 1 c. broth (or water) and juice from steamed chicken
　1/2 T. soy sauce
　1/2 t. sesame oil
③ { 1-1/2 t. cornstarch
　　1 T. water } mix

❶雞腿剁塊，香菇泡軟切塊，連同葱薑及①料醃 10 分鐘後，排入蒸碗中，水開大火蒸熟 (約 20 分鐘)，取出倒扣在盤上 (汁需先倒出留用)，青江菜煮熟圍邊。
❷將②料煮開，以③料勾芡，淋於雞上即成。

❶ Cut chicken legs into pieces. Soak mushrooms in cold water until soft and cut into pieces. Marinate chicken and mushrooms in green onion, ginger, and ① for 10 minutes. Place in bowl and steam over boiling water for 20 minutes or until done. Pour out liquid from bowl; retain liquid for ②. Invert bowl into serving plate. Blanch bok choy in boiling water until done and use as garnish for edge of serving plate.

❷ Bring ② to a boil, then thicken with ③. Pour over chicken and serve.

醬汁烹雞脯
CHICKEN BREAST WITH WORCESTERSHIRE SAUCE

營養含量 Nutritional Content		
蛋白質 Protein	（公克） (g)	9
脂　肪 Fat	（公克） (g)	12
醣 Carbohydrates	（公克） (g)	1
膽固醇 Cholesterol	（毫克） (mg)	26
熱　量 Calories	（大卡） (Cal)	148

1 人份　Per Serving

雞胸肉…………… 200 公克
　　　　　　　　（約 5½ 兩）
① 鹽………………… ¼ 小匙
　糖………………… 1 小匙
　酒………………… 1 小匙
　太白粉…………… 1 大匙
② 熟筍…… 30 公克（約 1 兩）
　紅蘿蔔…………… 30 公克
　蒜末……………… 1 小匙
③ 辣醬油…………… 2 大匙
　麻油……………… ½ 小匙
　糖………………… ½ 小匙
　沙拉油…………… 1 ½ 大匙

1/2 lb. (200 g.) chicken
　breast
1/4 t. salt
① 1 t. sugar
　1 t. cooking wine
　1 T. cornstarch
　1 oz. (30 g.) bamboo
② 　shoots (cooked)
　1 oz. (30 g.) carrots
　1 t. garlic (minced)
　2 T. worcestershire
③ 　sauce
　1/2 t. sesame oil
　1/2 t. sugar
　1-1/2 T. vegetable oil

❶雞肉切成 4×3×0.5 公分之薄片，加①料醃 10 分鐘，②料切花片。

❷油燒熱後，鍋離火將肉片排入，再置回爐上煎至兩面呈金黃色取出，餘油炒香蒜末，入③料煮開，下②料及肉片拌勻即刻起鍋。

■可以香菜點綴。

❶ Cut chicken meat into slices, 1-1/2'' x 1-1/4'' x 1/4''. Add ① and marinate for 10 minutes. Slice ② into flower shapes.

❷ Heat 1-1/2 T. oil in preheated wok. Remove wok from heat. Arrange meat on wok.Return wok to heat. Fry until both sides are golden. Remove from heat. In remaining oil, stir-fry minced garlic until fragrant. Add ③ and bring to a boil. Add ② and chicken slices; stir until mixed well. Remove from heat and serve.

■ Coriander may be used as garnish.

醬油鷄
CHICKEN IN SOY SAUCE

4 人份　Serves 4

營養含量 Nutritional Content		
蛋白質 Protein	（公克）(g)	9
脂　肪 Fat	（公克）(g)	14
醣 Carbohydrates	（公克）(g)	1
膽固醇 Cholesterol	（毫克）(mg)	36
熱　量 Calories	（大卡）(Cal)	166

1 人份　Per Serving

雞腿‥250 公克（約 6 ½ 兩）
葱（3 公分長）……… 6 段
薑絲……………… 1 大匙
① { 酒………………… 2 小匙
糖………………… 1 小匙
醬油……………… 2 大匙
水………………… 2 大匙
沙拉油…………… 2 大匙

1/2 lb. (250 g.) chicken
　legs
6 sections green onions
　(1-1/4")
1 T. shredded ginger
　root
① { 2 t. cooking wine
1 t. sugar
2 T. soy sauce
2 T. water
2 T. vegetable oil

❶葱、薑加①料拌勻，塗抹在擦乾水分的雞腿上，餘汁備用。

❷油 2 大匙燒至八分熱，入雞腿中火兩面各煎 10 秒鐘至外皮稍呈金黃色，隨下餘汁及水煮滾，改小火燜煮 20 分鐘（需時常翻面，以免燒焦），取出剁塊排盤，淋上醬汁即可。

■可以香菜、紅蘿蔔彩盤。

❶ Mix green onions and ginger with ①. Spread on chicken legs (which have been patted dry). Set aside remaining marinade.

❷ Heat 2 T. oil in preheated wok. Fry chicken legs over medium heat, 10 seconds on each side, or until both sides are slightly golden. Add remaining marinade and water. Bring to a boil. Reduce heat and simmer for 20 minutes (turn when necessary to avoid burning). Remove chicken. Chop into pieces and arrange on plate. Pour remaining juice over chicken and serve.

■ Coriander and carrot may be used as garnish.

鴛鴦綉球

MANDARIN MEATBALLS

4 人份　Serves 4

營養含量 Nutritional Content		
蛋白質　（公克） Protein　（g）	11
脂　肪　（公克） Fat　（g）	9
醣　　　（公克） Carbohydrates　（g）	4
膽固醇　（毫克） Cholesterol　（mg）	150
熱　量　（大卡） Calories　（Cal）	141

1 人份　Per Serving

蛋‥‥‥‥‥‥‥‥‥‥ 2 個
木耳‥‥‥‥ 75 公克（ 2 兩）
絞肉‥‥‥‥ 150 公克（ 4 兩）
荸薺‥‥‥ 70 公克（約 2 兩）
① 醬油‥‥‥‥‥‥‥‥ 1 小匙
　 鹽‥‥‥‥‥‥‥‥‥ 1/8 小匙
　 糖‥‥‥‥‥‥‥‥‥ 1/4 小匙
　 麻油‥‥‥‥‥‥‥‥ 1/2 小匙
　 薑酒汁‥‥‥‥‥‥‥ 1/2 小匙
　 太白粉‥‥‥‥‥‥‥ 1 小匙
② 蒸汁十高湯（或水）‥‥ 1 杯
　 鹽、糖‥‥‥‥‥‥ 各 1/4 小匙
　 胡椒 1/8 小匙、麻油 1/2 小匙
③ 太白粉‥‥‥‥‥‥ 1½ 小匙
　 水‥‥‥‥‥‥‥‥‥ 1 大匙

2 eggs
2-2/3 oz. (75 g.) soaked
　　wood ears
1/3 lb. (150 g.) ground
　　pork
2-1/2 oz. (70 g.) water
　　chestnuts
① 1 t. soy sauce
　 1/8 t. salt
　 1/4 t. sugar
　 1/2 t. sesame oil
　 1/2 t. ginger wine
　 1 t. cornstarch
② 1 c. broth (or water) and
　　juice from steamed
　　meatballs
　 1/4 t. each: salt, sugar
　 1/8 t. pepper
　 1/2 t. sesame oil
③ 1-1/2 t. cornstarch } mix
　 1 T. water

❶蛋 2 個打散，鍋抹油少許，小火煎成蛋皮切絲，木耳亦切絲，荸薺拍碎，擠乾水份備用。

❷絞肉、荸薺加①料仔細拌勻，擠成 18 個圓球，½ 裹上蛋絲，½ 裹上木耳絲置盤上，開水大火蒸 10 分鐘取出，蒸汁留用。

❸將②料煮開，並以③料勾芡，淋於肉丸上即成。

■可以炒熟的青菜墊盤底，增加美觀。

❶ Beat eggs. Thinly coat preheated wok with oil. Fry eggs over low heat to make thin omelet. Remove and cut into thin strips. Shred wood ear. Smash and mince water chestnuts, press out water with paper towel, and set aside.

❷ Add ① and water chestnuts to ground pork. Mix thoroughly. Form 18 round balls with ground pork mixture, adding soaked wood ear strips to nine meatballs and omelet strips to remaining nine. Steam meatballs on plate over boiling water for 10 minutes. Remove from heat. Pour off juice and set aside.

❸ Bring ② to a boil. Thicken with ③. Pour over meatballs and serve.

■ Cooked green vegetables may be arranged under the meatballs as garnish.

番茄燒鴨塊 STEWED DUCK AND TOMATO

營養含量 Nutritional Content		
蛋白質 Protein	（公克）(g)	10
脂 肪 Fat	（公克）(g)	12
醣 Carbohydrates	（公克）(g)	4
膽固醇 Cholesterol	（毫克）(mg)	31
熱 量 Calories	（大卡）(Cal)	164

1 人份　Per Serving

鴨···· 350 公克（約 9 ½ 兩）
太白粉················· 2 小匙
番茄··200 公克（約 5 ½ 兩）
① 　葱（3 公分長）········· 3 段
　　薑················· 3 片
　　蒜頭（拍碎）············· 3 粒
② 　醬油················· 2 小匙
　　酒················· 1 小匙
　　鹽················· ⅓ 小匙
　　胡椒················· ⅛ 小匙
　　水················· 1 ¼ 杯
番茄醬··············· 2 大匙
沙拉油··············· 1 ½ 大匙

3/4 lb. (350 g.) duck
2 t. cornstarch
1/2 lb. (200 g.) tomatoes
① 　3 sections green onions,
　　　1-1/4" long
　　3 slices ginger root
　　3 cloves garlic,
　　　(crushed)
② 　2 t. soy sauce
　　1 t. cooking wine
　　1/3 t. salt
　　1/8 t. pepper
　　1-1/4 c. water
2 T. ketchup
1-1/2 T. vegetable oil

❶鴨剁成 4 公分方塊，加太白粉拌勻，番茄切塊狀。

❷油 1 ½ 大匙燒熱，將①料炒香，入鴨塊炒至變色，再下番茄及②料大火煮滾，改小火燜煮 20 分鐘，加番茄醬再煮 5 分鐘即可盛盤。

■可加上葱絲點綴，鴨肉亦可改用雞肉。

❶ Chop duck into 1-1/2" squares. Add 2 t. cornstarch and mix. Cut tomatoes into pieces.

❷ Heat 1-1/2 T. oil in preheated wok. Stir-fry ① until fragrant. Add duck and stir-fry until color changes. Mix in tomatoes and ②. Bring to a boil. Reduce heat and simmer for 20 minutes. Add 2 T. ketchup and simmer for 5 more minutes. Serve.

■ Shredded green onion may be sprinkled on duck for embellishment. Chicken may be substituted for duck.

醬味肉絲拌芽菜
PORK STRIPS AND RADISH SPROUTS

營養含量 Nutritional Content		
蛋白質 Protein	（公克） (g)	9
脂　肪 Fat	（公克） (g)	14
醣 Carbohydrates	（公克） (g)	1
膽固醇 Cholesterol	（毫克） (mg)	33
熱　量 Calories	（大卡） (Cal)	162

1 人份　Per Serving

里肌肉············· 200 公克
（約 5 ½ 兩）

① 醬油················· 1 小匙
酒··················· ½ 小匙
太白粉··············· 2 小匙
水··················· 1 小匙

貝芽菜(蘿蔔嬰)··· 50 公克
（約 1 ½ 兩）

② 甜麵醬··············· 2 小匙
醬油················· 1 小匙
麻油················· ½ 小匙
酒··················· 1 小匙
糖··················· ½ 小匙
水··················· 1 大匙
太白粉··············· ½ 小匙

沙拉油··············· 2 大匙

1/2 lb. (200 g.) pork loin

① 1 t. soy sauce
1/2 t. cooking wine
2 t. cornstarch
1 t. water

1-3/4 oz. (50 g.) white
radish sprouts

② 2 t. sweet bean paste
1 t. soy sauce
1/2 t. sesame oil
1 t. cooking wine
1/2 t. sugar
1 T. water
1/2 t. cornstarch

2 T. vegetable oil

❶里肌肉切絲，以①料醃 10 分鐘，貝芽菜鋪於盤內。

❷油 2 大匙燒熱，下肉絲炒至變色取出，餘油將攪勻之②料炒香，隨入肉絲炒勻盛於芽菜上，食時加以攪拌即可。

■貝芽菜(蘿蔔種子所長的嫩芽)可改用小黃瓜絲替代。

❶ Cut pork loin into strips. Marinate in ① for 10 minutes. Arrange white radish sprouts on plate.

❷ Heat 2 T. oil in preheated wok. Stir-fry pork strips until color changes; remove. In remaining oil, stir-fry evenly-mixed ② until fragrant; add pork and mix well. Remove pork and arrange over white radish sprouts; mix together when ready to serve.

■Gherkin cucumber strips may be substituted for white radish sprouts.

紅燒排骨　SPARERIBS COOKED IN SOY SAUCE

4 人份　Serves 4

營養含量 Nutritional Content		
蛋白質 Protein	（公克） (g)	11
脂　肪 Fat	（公克） (g)	8
醣 Carbohydrates	（公克） (g)	10
膽固醇 Cholesterol	（毫克） (mg)	38
熱　量 Calories	（大卡） (Cal)	156

1 人份　Per Serving

小排骨⋯⋯ 300 公克（8 兩）
紅蘿蔔⋯⋯ 150 公克（4 兩）
① 水⋯⋯⋯⋯⋯⋯⋯ ½ 杯
醬油⋯⋯⋯⋯⋯⋯ 3 大匙
糖⋯⋯⋯⋯⋯⋯⋯ 2 大匙
醋⋯⋯⋯⋯⋯⋯⋯ 2 大匙
酒⋯⋯⋯⋯⋯⋯⋯ 1 大匙

2/3 lb. (300 g.) spareribs
1/3 lb. (150 g.) carrots
① 1/2 c. water
3 T. soy sauce
2 T. sugar
2 T. vinegar
1 T. cooking wine

❶小排骨切 3 公分長段，紅蘿蔔切滾刀塊。

❷①料煮開，入小排骨、紅蘿蔔大火煮開，改小火燜煮 40 分鐘即可盛盤。
亦可撒少許蔥絲以增美觀。

❶ Cut ribs into 1-1/4″ long sections. Cut carrots into pieces.

❷ Bring ① to a boil. Add spareribs and carrots. Bring to another boil.
Reduce heat and simmer for 40 minutes. Serve.

■ Shredded green onion may be used as garnish.

南乳烤排骨 BAKED PORK RIBS

4 人份　Serves 4

營養含量 Nutritional Content		
蛋白質 Protein	（公克） (g)	13
脂　肪 Fat	（公克） (g)	10
醣 Carbohydrates	（公克） (g)	1
膽固醇 Cholesterol	（毫克） (mg)	45
熱　量 Calories	（大卡） (Cal)	142

1 人份　Per Serving

小排骨············ 350 公克
　　　　　　　（約 9½ 兩）
　豆腐乳················ 1 大匙
　糖····················· ½ 小匙
①　醬油················· 1 大匙
　麻油················· 1 小匙
　胡椒················· ¼ 小匙
　蒜泥················· 1 大匙

3/4 lb. (350 g.) pork ribs
　1 T. preserved bean curd
　1/2 t. sugar
①　1 T. soy sauce
　1 t. sesame oil
　1/4 t. pepper
　1 T. garlic paste

❶小排骨切約 5 公分長條狀，以①料拌醃 1 小時。

❷烤箱燒熱，排骨以 450°F 烤 30 分鐘即可（每 10 分鐘翻面一次，並抹上醃排骨之調味汁）。

■豆腐乳可用薄鹽味噌取代。

■可以番茄、巴西利、高麗菜等彩盤。

❶ Cut pork ribs into 2″ long pieces. Marinate in ① for one hour.

❷ Pre-heat oven. Bake pork ribs at 450 degrees for 30 minutes (turn and brush with marinade every 10 minutes). Serve.

■Mild miso paste may be substituted for preserved bean curd.

■Tomatoes, parsley and cabbage may be used as garnish.

蒜香里肌　GARLIC-FLAVORED PORK

營養含量 Nutritional Content		
蛋白質 Protein	（公克） (g)	11
脂 肪 Fat	（公克） (g)	11
醣 Carbohydrates	（公克） (g)	—
膽固醇 Cholesterol	（毫克） (mg)	38
熱 量 Calories	（大卡） (Cal)	143

1 人份　Per Serving

里肌肉····· 225 公克（6 兩）
① {
醬油····················· 1 大匙
酒、糖、麻油···· 各 ½ 小匙
太白粉················· 2 小匙
蒜末················· 2 小匙
}
沙拉油················ 1 大匙

1/2 lb. (225 g.) pork loin
① {
1 T. soy sauce
1/2 t. cooking wine
1/2 t. sugar
1/2 t. sesame oil
2 t. cornstarch
2 t. garlic (minced)
}
1 T. vegetable oil

❶里肌肉切約 0.5 公分厚片拍鬆，加①料拌醃 10 分鐘。

❷油 1 大匙燒熱，將肉片以中火兩面煎黃至熟即可。

■可以紅蘿蔔花、巴西利彩盤。

❶ Cut pork loin into slices, 1/4″ thick. Tenderize pork with meat mallet. Add ① and marinate for 10 minutes.

❷ Heat 1 T. oil in preheated wok. Fry pork slices until brown on both sides or until done. Remove and serve

■Flower-shaped carrot slices and parsley may be used as garnish.

醬爆四寶
RAINBOW VEGETABLES AND GROUND BEEF

4 人份　Serves 4

營養含量 Nutritional Content		
蛋白質 Protein	（公克） (g)	9
脂　肪 Fat	（公克） (g)	14
醣 Carbohydrates	（公克） (g)	1
膽固醇 Cholesterol	（毫克） (mg)	27
熱　量 Calories	（大卡） (Cal)	166

1 人份　Per Serving

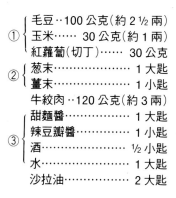

① 毛豆‧‧100 公克(約 2 ½ 兩)
　玉米‧‧‧‧‧‧ 30 公克(約 1 兩)
　紅蘿蔔(切丁)‧‧‧‧‧‧ 30 公克
② 葱末‧‧‧‧‧‧‧‧‧‧‧‧‧‧ 1 大匙
　薑末‧‧‧‧‧‧‧‧‧‧‧‧‧‧ 1 小匙
　牛絞肉‧‧120 公克(約 3 兩)
③ 甜麵醬‧‧‧‧‧‧‧‧‧‧‧‧ 1 大匙
　辣豆瓣醬‧‧‧‧‧‧‧‧‧ 1 小匙
　酒‧‧‧‧‧‧‧‧‧‧‧‧‧‧‧‧ ½ 小匙
　水‧‧‧‧‧‧‧‧‧‧‧‧‧‧‧‧ 1 大匙
　沙拉油‧‧‧‧‧‧‧‧‧‧‧‧ 2 大匙

① 3-1/2 oz. (100 g.) fresh
　soy beans or peas
　1 oz. (30 g.) corn
　1 oz. (30 g.) carrots
　(cubed)
② 1 T. green onion
　(minced)
　ginger root (minced)
　1/4 lb. (120 g.) ground
　beef
③ 1 T. sweet bean paste
　1 t. hot bean paste
　1/2 t. cooking wine
　1 T. water
　2 T. vegetable oil

❶將①料以滾水煮熟取出備用。

❷油 2 大匙燒熱，炒香②料，入牛絞肉炒至變色，再下③料炒香，並加①料炒勻即可。

❶ Boil ① until done. Remove and set aside.

❷ Heat 2 T. oil in preheated wok. Stir-fry② until fragrant. Add ground beef and stir-fry until color changes. Add ③ and stir-fry until fragrant. Add ① and stir to mix. Remove from heat and serve.

肉片黃瓜捲 PORK STRIP CUCUMBER ROLLS

4 人份　Serves 4

營養含量 Nutritional Content		
蛋白質 Protein	（公克） (g)	11
脂 肪 Fat	（公克） (g)	8
醣 Carbohydrates	（公克） (g)	9
膽固醇 Cholesterol	（毫克） (mg)	38
熱 量 Calories	（大卡） (Cal)	152

1 人份　Per Serving

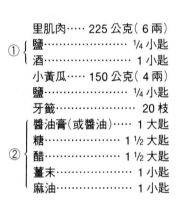

里肌肉‥‥‥ 225 公克（6 兩）
① ┌ 鹽‥‥‥‥‥‥‥‥‥ ¼ 小匙
　 └ 酒‥‥‥‥‥‥‥‥‥ 1 小匙
小黃瓜‥‥‥ 150 公克（4 兩）
　 鹽‥‥‥‥‥‥‥‥‥ ¼ 小匙
牙籤‥‥‥‥‥‥‥‥ 20 枝
　 醬油膏（或醬油）‥‥‥ 1 大匙
　 糖‥‥‥‥‥‥‥‥ 1 ½ 大匙
② ┤ 醋‥‥‥‥‥‥‥‥ 1 ½ 大匙
　 薑末‥‥‥‥‥‥‥‥ 1 小匙
　 麻油‥‥‥‥‥‥‥‥ 1 小匙

① { 1/2 lb. (225 g.) pork loin
　 1/4 t. salt
　 1 t. cooking wine
　 1/3 lb. (150 g.) gherkin
　　 cucumbers
　 1/4 t. salt
　 20 toothpicks
② { 1 T. soy sauce paste or
　　 soy sauce
　 1-1/2 T. sugar
　 1-1/2 T. vinegar
　 1 t. ginger (minced)
　 1 t. sesame oil

❶肉抹上①料蒸熟約 20 分鐘，切 4×7×0.2 公分薄片（共 16 片）。

❷小黃瓜切成 2 段，再切 0.1 公分厚之長薄片（32 片），以鹽 ¼ 小匙醃 10 分鐘至軟。

❸取二片黃瓜夾一片肉捲成筒狀，用牙籤穿好固定，食時沾上拌勻的②料即可。

■可以番茄、巴西利、高麗菜等彩盤。

■小黃瓜片亦可以生菜代替。

❶ Rub① on pork and steam for approximately 20 minutes until done. Slice meat into 16 thin slices, 2-3/4″ x 1-1/2″ x 1/12″.

❷ Slice cucumbers in half, then slice lengthwise into about 32 thin slices, 1/25″ thick. Add 1/4 t. salt and pickle for 10 minutes until soft.

❸ Place one meat slice between 2 cucumber slices. Roll and secure with toothpick. Before eating, dip rolls into evenly mixed②.

■ Tomatoes, parsley, and cabbage may be used as garnish.

■ Lettuce may be substituted for gherkin cucumbers.

玉蘭牛肉　CHINESE BROCCOLI AND BEEF

4 人份　Serves 4

營養含量 Nutritional Content		
蛋白質 Protein	（公克）(g)	9
脂 肪 Fat	（公克）(g)	14
醣 Carbohydrates	（公克）(g)	1
膽固醇 Cholesterol	（毫克）(mg)	44
熱 量 Calories	（大卡）(Cal)	166

1 人份　Per Serving

牛里肌肉‥‥‥‥‥ 200 公克
　　　　　　　（約 5 ½ 兩）
① 酒‥‥‥‥‥‥‥‥‥ 2 小匙
　 醬油‥‥‥‥‥‥‥‥ 1 大匙
　 太白粉‥‥‥‥‥‥‥ 2 小匙
油‥‥‥‥‥‥‥‥‥‥ 1 小匙
葱（3 公分長）‥‥‥‥ 3 段
薑‥‥‥‥‥‥‥‥‥‥ 3 片
② 玉米筍（煮熟）‥‥‥ 50 公克
　 芥蘭菜 50 公克（約 1 ½ 兩）
　 紅蘿蔔（煮熟）‥‥‥ 30 公克
　　　　　　　　（約 1 兩）
③ 酒‥1 小匙、醬油‥1 大匙
　 糖、麻油‥‥‥‥‥ 各 ½ 小匙
　 太白粉‥‥‥‥‥‥‥ 1 小匙
　 水‥‥‥‥‥‥‥‥‥ 3 大匙
沙拉油‥‥‥‥‥‥‥‥ 2 大匙

1/2 lb. (200 g.) beef loin
　(or flank steak)
① 2 t. cooking wine
　 1 T. soy sauce
　 2 t. cornstarch
1 t. vegetable oil
3 section green onion
3 slices ginger root
② 1-3/4 oz. (50 g.) baby
　 corn (cooked)
　 1-3/4 oz.(50 g.) Chinese
　 broccoli
　 1 oz. (30 g.) carrots
　 (cooked)
③ 1 t. cooking wine
　 1 T. soy sauce
　 1/2 t. sugar
　 1/2 t. sesame oil
　 1 t. cornstarch
　 3 T. water
2 T. vegetable oil

❶牛肉切薄片，加①料醃 10 分鐘。炒前加油 1 小匙拌勻（肉較易鏟開），芥蘭菜切段，紅蘿蔔切片。

❷油燒熱，入肉片中火炒至變色即刻撈出，餘油炒香葱、薑，隨入②料、牛肉及③料大火炒勻即可。

❶ Thinly slice beef. Add ① and marinate for 10 minutes. Add 1t. oil to beef and mix evenly before stir-frying for easy separation. Cut Chinese broccoli into sections. Slice carrots.

❷ Heat 2 T. oil in preheated wok. Stir-fry beef over medium heat until brown. Remove immediately. In remaining oil, stir-fry green onion and ginger until fragrant. Add ②, beef, and ③; stir-fry over high heat until mixed well. Remove from heat and serve.

嫩薑炒羊肉
STIR-FRIED LAMB AND BABY GINGER ROOT

4 人份　Serves 4

營養含量 Nutritional Content		
蛋白質 Protein	（公克）(g)	9
脂 肪 Fat	（公克）(g)	14
醣 Carbohydrates	（公克）(g)	1
膽固醇 Cholesterol	（毫克）(mg)	49
熱 量 Calories	（大卡）(Cal)	162

1 人份　Per Serving

羊肉片⋯⋯⋯⋯ 200 公克
　　　　　　　（約 5 ½ 兩）
① {
酒⋯⋯⋯⋯⋯⋯ 1 小匙
醬油⋯⋯⋯⋯⋯ 2 小匙
太白粉⋯⋯⋯⋯ 2 小匙
胡椒⋯⋯⋯⋯⋯ ⅛ 小匙
麻油⋯⋯⋯⋯⋯ ½ 小匙
}
② {
嫩薑絲⋯⋯⋯⋯ 3 大匙
紅辣椒絲⋯⋯⋯ 1 大匙
葱絲⋯⋯⋯⋯⋯ ½ 杯
}
沙拉油⋯⋯⋯⋯ 3 大匙

1/2 lb. (200 g.) lamb
 (sliced)
① {
1 t. cooking wine
2 t. soy sauce
2 t. cornstarch
1/8 t. pepper
1/2 t. sesame oil
}
② {
3 T. shredded baby
 ginger root
1 T. shredded red chili
 pepper
1/2 c. shredded green
 onion
}
3 T. vegetable oil

❶羊肉片加①料拌勻醃 10 分鐘。

❷油 3 大匙燒熱，入羊肉中火炒至變色取出，餘油炒香②料，隨入羊肉炒勻即可。

■羊肉可用牛肉代替，如無嫩薑絲亦可改用老薑 1 ½ 大匙。

❶ Add ① to sliced lamb and marinate for 10 minutes.

❷ Heat 3 T. oil in preheated wok. Add lamb and stir-fry over medium heat until color changes. Remove from heat. In remaining oil, stir-fry ② until fragrant; add lamb and mix well. Remove from heat and serve.

■ Beef may be substituted for lamb. If baby ginger root is unavailable, 1-1/2 T. shredded ginger root may be used as substitute.

鮮蓮子鷄丁 LOTUS SEEDS AND CHICKEN CUBES

營養含量 Nutritional Content		
蛋白質 Protein	（公克） (g)	5
脂　肪 Fat	（公克） (g)	10
醣 Carbohydrates	（公克） (g)	8
膽固醇 Cholesterol	（毫克） (mg)	14
熱　量 Calories	（大卡） (Cal)	142

1 人份　Per Serving

雞胸肉⋯⋯ 75 公克（ 2 兩）
① 鹽⋯⋯⋯⋯⋯⋯ ¼ 小匙
　 酒⋯⋯⋯⋯⋯⋯ ½ 小匙
　 太白粉⋯⋯⋯⋯⋯ 1 小匙
② 香菇(泡軟)⋯⋯⋯⋯ 3 朵
　 豌豆夾⋯ 30 公克（約 1 兩）
　 熟紅蘿蔔⋯⋯⋯⋯ 30 公克
鮮蓮子⋯120 公克（約 3 兩）
葱（ 3 公分長）⋯⋯⋯ 3 段
③ 酒⋯⋯⋯⋯⋯⋯ ½ 小匙
　 鹽⋯⋯⋯⋯⋯⋯ ¼ 小匙
　 麻油⋯⋯⋯⋯⋯⋯ ½ 小匙
　 太白粉⋯⋯⋯⋯⋯ 1 小匙
　 水⋯⋯⋯⋯⋯⋯ 3 大匙
沙拉油⋯⋯⋯⋯⋯⋯ 2 大匙

2-2/3 oz. (75 g.) chicken
　breast
① 1/4 t. salt
　 1/2 t. cooking wine
　 1 t. cornstarch
② 3 Chinese black
　　mushrooms (soaked)
　 1 oz. (30 g.) each: snow
　　peas (Chinese pea
　　pods), carrots (cooked)
4-1/4 oz. (120 g.) fresh
　lotus seeds
3 sections green onion
　(1-1/4'')
③ 1/2 t. each: cooking
　　wine, sesame oil
　 1/4 t. salt
　 1 t. cornstarch
　 3 T. water
2 T. vegetable oil

❶雞肉切 1.5 公分方丁，加①料醃 10 分鐘。

❷②料切菱形片，鮮蓮子以滾水煮熟(約 4 分鐘)撈出，瀝乾水分備用。

❸油燒熱，爆香葱段，入雞丁炒至變色，隨入②料炒數下，再下③料及蓮子炒勻即可。

❶ Cut chicken breast into 2/3'' cubes, add ① and marinate for 10 minutes.

❷ Cut ② into pieces. Boil lotus seeds until done (approx. 4 minutes). Remove lotus seeds. Drain off water and set aside.

❸ Heat 2 T. oil in preheated wok. Stir-fry green onion sections until fragrant. Add chicken cubes and stir-fry until color changes. Add ② and quickly stir-fry. Add ③ and lotus seeds; stir-fry until mixed well. Remove from heat and serve.

豌豆鷄絲 PEAS AND CHICKEN STRIPS

營養含量 Nutritional Content		
蛋白質 Protein	（公克） (g)	5
脂　肪 Fat	（公克） (g)	10
醣 Carbohydrates	（公克） (g)	3
膽固醇 Cholesterol	（毫克） (mg)	14
熱　量 Calories	（大卡） (Cal)	122

1 人份　Per Serving

雞胸肉……　75 公克（ 2 兩）
① 鹽………………… ⅙ 小匙
酒………………… 1 小匙
蛋白………………… ½ 個
太白粉……………… 1 大匙
葱花………………… 1 大匙
熟豌豆……… 200 公克
（約 5 ½ 兩）
② 鹽………………… ¼ 小匙
麻油……………… ¼ 小匙
沙拉油…………… 2 大匙

2-2/3 oz. (75 g.) chicken
　breast
① 1/6 t. salt
1 t. cooking wine
1/2 egg white
1 T. cornstarch
1 T. green onion
　(chopped)
7 oz. (200 g.) peas
　(cooked)
② 1/4 t. salt
1/4 t. sesame oil
2 T. vegetable oil

❶雞胸肉切絲，加①料拌勻醃 10 分鐘。

❷油燒至八分熱，雞絲中火炒至變白撈起，餘油炒香葱花，隨入豌豆、雞絲及②料炒勻即可。

■豌豆也可用玉米、嫩蠶豆、毛豆等取代。

❶ Cut chicken breast into strips. Add ① and marinate for 10 minutes.

❷ Heat 2 T. oil in preheated wok . Stir-fry chicken over medium heat until white. Remove from heat. In remaining oil, stir-fry green onion until fragrant. Add peas, chicken, and ②. Mix evenly and remove from heat.

■ Corn and lima beans may be substituted for peas.

海帶捲　SEAWEED PORK ROLLS

4 人份　Serves 4

營養含量 Nutritional Content		
蛋白質 Protein	（公克）(g)	5
脂肪 Fat	（公克）(g)	3
醣 Carbohydrates	（公克）(g)	16
膽固醇 Cholesterol	（毫克）(mg)	13
熱量 Calories	（大卡）(Cal)	111

1 人份　Per Serving

海帶（泡軟）‧‧‧‧‧‧‧ 200 公克
　　　　　　（約 5 ½ 兩）
里肌肉‧‧‧‧‧‧ 75 公克（2 兩）

① {
醬油‧‧‧‧‧‧‧‧‧‧‧‧‧‧‧ 1 小匙
糖‧‧‧‧‧‧‧‧‧‧‧‧‧‧‧‧‧ ½ 小匙
酒‧‧‧‧‧‧‧‧‧‧‧‧‧‧‧‧‧ ½ 小匙
太白粉‧‧‧‧‧‧‧‧‧‧‧‧ 1 小匙
}

干瓢‧‧‧‧‧‧‧‧‧‧‧‧‧ 150 公分

② {
紅蘿蔔‧‧‧ 30 公克（約 1 兩）
筍‧‧‧‧‧‧‧‧‧‧‧‧‧‧‧‧ 30 公克
香菇（泡軟）‧‧‧‧‧‧‧‧ 3 朵
}

③ {
水‧‧‧‧‧‧‧‧‧‧‧‧‧‧‧‧‧‧ 2 杯
糖‧‧‧‧‧‧‧‧‧‧‧‧‧‧‧‧‧ 3 大匙
醋‧‧‧‧‧‧‧‧‧‧‧‧‧‧‧‧‧ 3 大匙
醬油‧‧‧‧‧‧‧‧‧‧‧‧‧‧ 3 大匙
蒜頭（拍碎）‧‧‧‧‧‧‧‧ 6 瓣
}

1/2 lb. (200 g.) seaweed
　(soaked)
2-2/3 oz. (75 g.) pork loin

① {
1 t. soy sauce
1/2 t. sugar
1/2 t. cooking wine
1 t. cornstarch
}

60″ dried gourd
　shavings

② {
1 oz. (30 g.) carrots
1 oz. (30 g.) bamboo
　shoots
3 Chinese black
　mushrooms (soaked)
}

③ {
2 c. water
3 T. sugar
3 T. vinegar
3 T. soy sauce
6 cloves garlic
　(crushed)
}

❶海帶橫切 5 公分長段，里肌肉亦切 5 公分長薄片，加①料醃 10 分鐘，干瓢泡軟切成 12 公分長段，②料切成 5 公分長條狀（各 12 份）。

❷取海帶一片，上鋪肉片，並放一份②料捲成筒狀，以干瓢綁緊，依次做好共 12 捲。

❸將③料煮開，入海帶捲待滾，改小火燜煮約 30 分鐘即可。

■可以紅蘿蔔、巴西利彩盤。

❶ Cut seaweed into sections, 2″ long. Also cut pork loin into slices, 2″ long. Add ① and marinate for 10 minutes. Soak dried gourd shavings in water until soft. Cut into sections, 5″ long. Cut ② into sticks, 2″ long (12 of each).

❷ Place one pork strip on one seaweed strip. Then place one serving amount of ② on top of pork strip and roll. Tie each roll tightly with gourd shaving. Repeat until 12 rolls have been made.

❸ Bring ③ to a boil. Add seaweed rolls and bring to another boil. Reduce heat and simmer for about 30 minutes. Serve.

■ Carrots and parsley may be used as garnish.

雙菇肉片
STIR-FRIED MEAT SLICES WITH MUSHROOMS

營養含量 Nutritional Content		
蛋白質 Protein	（公克） (g)	4
脂　肪 Fat	（公克） (g)	10
醣 Carbohydrates	（公克） (g)	2
膽固醇 Cholesterol	（毫克） (mg)	13
熱　量 Calories	（大卡） (Cal)	114

1 人份　Per Serving

里肌肉…… 75 公克（2 兩）
① 酒……………………… ½ 小匙
　醬油………………… ½ 小匙
　太白粉……………… ½ 小匙
② 洋菇… 50 公克（約 1 ½ 兩）
　草菇……… 75 公克（2 兩）
　筍……………………… 50 公克
　紅蘿蔔… 30 公克（約 1 兩）
　葱（3 公分長）……… 3 段
③ 鹽………………………… ¼ 小匙
　糖………………………… ½ 小匙
　麻油…………………… ½ 小匙
　太白粉……………… ⅔ 小匙
　水……………………… 3 大匙
　沙拉油………………… 2 大匙

2-2/3 oz. (75 g.) pork loin
① 1/2 t. cooking wine
　1/2 t. soy sauce
　1/2 t. cornstarch
② 1-3/4 oz. (50 g.) button
　　mushrooms
　2-2/3 oz. (75 g.) straw
　　mushrooms
　1-3/4 oz. (50 g.) bamboo
　　shoots
　1 oz. (30 g.) carrots
　3 sections green onions
　　(1-1/4'')
③ 1/4 t. salt
　1/2 t. sugar
　1/2 t. sesame oil
　2/3 t. cornstarch
　3 T. water
　2 T. vegetable oil

❶里肌肉切薄片，加①料拌勻，②料燙熟切片。

❷油燒熱，入肉片炒至變色，隨入葱段炒香，再下②料炒數下，以③料調味並炒勻即可。

❶ Thinly slice pork loin. Add ① and mix evenly. Quickly boil ② and remove from heat. Slice.

❷ Heat 2 T. oil in preheated wok. Add meat slices and stir-fry until color changes. Add green onion sections and stir-fry until fragrant. Add ② and quickly stir-fry. Add ③ and stir-fry until mixed well. Remove from heat. Serve.

生菜拌燒肉
BARBECUED PORK AND LETTUCE SALAD

4 人份　Serves 4

營養含量 Nutritional Content		
蛋白質 Protein	（公克） (g)	5
脂　肪 Fat	（公克） (g)	9
醣 Carbohydrates	（公克） (g)	3
膽固醇 Cholesterol	（毫克） (mg)	15
熱　量 Calories	（大卡） (Cal)	113

1 人份　Per Serving

　叉燒肉……75 公克(2 兩)

① ｛ 包生菜…………… 100 公克
（約 2½ 兩）
紅蘿蔔 50 公克(約 1½ 兩)
洋葱…… 20 公克(約 ½ 兩)
青椒…… 30 公克(約 1 兩)

② ｛ 芝麻醬……………… 1 大匙
醬油………………… 1 小匙
糖………………… 1 小匙
醋………………… 1 小匙
麻油……………… 1 大匙
水……………… 1 大匙

2-2/3 oz. (75 g.)
　barbecued pork

① ｛ 1/4 lb. (100 g.) lettuce
1-3/4 oz. (50 g.) carrots
3/4 oz. (20 g.) onions
1 oz. (30 g.) green
　pepper

② ｛ 1 T. sesame paste
1 t. soy sauce
1 t. sugar
1 t. vinegar
1 T. sesame oil
1 T. water

❶叉燒肉切成絲，①料亦切絲，②料調勻備用。

❷叉燒肉及①料拌勻盛盤上，食時淋上②料即可。

■叉燒肉可改用白切肉、雞肉或燒鴨肉。

❶ Cut barbecued pork into strips. Also cut ① into strips. Mix ② and set aside.

❷ Mix barbecued pork and ①. Arrange on a serving plate. Pour ② over pork mixture. Mix and serve.

■ Boiled pork, baked chicken, or baked duck may be substituted for barbecued pork.

木耳炒鳳梨
STIR-FRIED WOOD EARS AND PINEAPPLE

4 人份　Serves 4

營養含量 Nutritional Content		
蛋白質 Protein	（公克） (g)	4
脂　肪 Fat	（公克） (g)	10
醣 Carbohydrates	（公克） (g)	6
膽固醇 Cholesterol	（毫克） (mg)	13
熱　量 Calories	（大卡） (Cal)	130

1 人份　Per Serving

木耳……… 150 公克（ 4 兩）
鳳梨……………… 150 公克
里肌肉…… 75 公克（ 2 兩）
① 醬油……………… ¼ 小匙
　 太白粉…………… ½ 小匙
② 葱（ 3 公分長）…… 5 段
　 薑………………… 2 片
　 紅辣椒（去籽切片）…… 1 條
③ 醬油……………… 1 小匙
　 鹽………………… ¼ 小匙
　 糖………………… ½ 小匙
　 鳳梨汁…………… ½ 杯
④ 太白粉…………… ½ 小匙
　 水………………… 1 大匙
　 沙拉油…………… 2 大匙

1/3 lb. (150 g.) soaked
　 wood ears
1/3 lb. (150 g.) pineapple
2-2/3 oz. (75 g.) pork loin
① { 1/4 t. soy sauce
　　 1/2 t. cornstarch
② { 5 sections green onion
　　　 (1-1/4")
　　 2 slices ginger root
　　 1 red chili pepper
　　　 (seeded, sliced)
③ { 1 t. soy sauce
　　 1/4 t. salt
　　 1/2 t. sugar
　　 1/2 c. pineapple juice
④ { 1/2 t. cornstarch
　　 1 T. water　} mix
　　 2 T. vegetable oil

❶木耳、鳳梨切片，里肌肉切薄片加①料。

❷油 2 大匙燒熱，②料炒香，下肉片炒至八分熟，再下木耳、鳳梨拌炒，入③料煮滾，再以④料勾芡即可。

■鳳梨可用新鮮的或罐頭均可。

❶ Slice wood ears and pineapple. Thinly slice pork loin and marinate in ①.

❷ Heat 2 T. oil in preheated wok. Stir-fry ② until fragrant. Add pork slices and stir-fry until color changes. Add wood ears and pineapple; stir to mix. Add ③ and bring to a boil. Thicken with ④ and serve.

■Fresh or canned pineapple may be used.

芫爆里肌　BEEF AND BAMBOO SHOOTS

營養含量 Nutritional Content		
蛋白質 Protein	（公克）(g)	4
脂 肪 Fat	（公克）(g)	10
醣 Carbohydrates	（公克）(g)	2
膽固醇 Cholesterol	（毫克）(mg)	17
熱 量 Calories	（大卡）(Cal)	114

1 人份　Per Serving

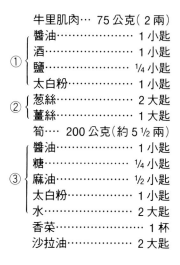

牛里肌肉… 75 公克(2 兩)
① 醬油……………… 1 小匙
　 酒………………… 1 小匙
　 鹽………………… ¼ 小匙
　 太白粉…………… 1 小匙
② 葱絲……………… 2 大匙
　 薑絲……………… 1 大匙
筍…… 200 公克(約 5 ½ 兩)
③ 醬油……………… 1 小匙
　 糖………………… ¼ 小匙
　 麻油……………… ½ 小匙
　 太白粉…………… 1 小匙
　 水………………… 2 大匙
香菜………………… 1 杯
沙拉油……………… 2 大匙

2-2/3 oz. (75 g.) beef loin
　(or flank steak)
① 1 t. soy sauce
　 1 t. cooking wine
　 1/4 t. salt
　 1 t. cornstarch
② 2 T. shredded green
　　onion
　 1 T. shredded ginger
　　root
　 1/2 lb. (200 g.)
　　bamboo shoots
③ 1 t. soy sauce
　 1/4 t. sugar
　 1/2 t. sesame oil
　 1 t. cornstarch
　 2 T. water
　 1 c. coriander
　 2 T. vegetable oil

❶牛肉橫紋切絲加①料醃 10 分鐘，筍加水煮 20 分鐘待冷切絲。

❷油 2 大匙燒熱，入牛肉中火炒至變色即刻撈出，餘油炒香②料，隨入筍絲、牛肉、③料及香菜速炒勻即可。

■如無香菜可免用，可加紅椒絲點綴。

❶ Cut beef against the grain into strips. Add ① and marinate for 10 minutes. Place bamboo shoots in cold water and bring to a boil. Cook for 20 minutes and cut into strips when cool.

❷ Heat 2 T. oil in preheated wok. Stir-fry beef over medium heat until color changes. Remove from heat. In remaining oil, stir-fry ② until fragrant. Add bamboo shoots, beef, ③, and coriander; stir-fry until mixed. Remove from heat and serve.

■ Coriander may be omitted if unavailable. Shredded red chili pepper may be used as garnish.

清炒鷄絲　STIR-FRIED CHICKEN STRIPS

營養含量 Nutritional Content		
蛋白質　（公克） Protein　（g）		4
脂　肪　（公克） Fat　（g）		10
醣　　　（公克） Carbohydrates　（g）		2
膽固醇　（毫克） Cholesterol　（mg）		14
熱　量　（大卡） Calories　（Cal）		114

1 人份　Per Serving

雞胸淨肉… 75 公克（ 2 兩）
① 酒……………………… 2 小匙
　 醬油………………… 1/4 小匙
　 太白粉……………… 2 小匙
② 香菇……………………… 4 朵
　 薑絲、葱絲……… 各 1 大匙
　 蒜末…………………… 1 小匙
③ 熟筍絲………………… 100 公克
　　　　　　　（約 2½ 兩）
　 青椒絲………………… 100 公克
　　　　　　　（約 2½ 兩）
　 紅椒絲…10 公克（約 ⅓ 兩）
④ 酒……………………… 1 小匙
　 鹽、麻油……… 各 ½ 小匙
　 太白粉……………… 1 小匙
　 水…………………… 2 大匙
沙拉油……………… 2 大匙

2-2/3 oz. (75 g.) chicken
　breast (boned,
　skinned)
① 2 t. cooking wine
　 1/4 t. soy sauce
　 2 t. cornstarch
② 4 Chinese black
　　mushrooms
　 1 T. ginger (strips)
　 1 T. green onion (strips)
　 1 t. garlic (minced)
③ 1/4 lb. (100 g.) bamboo
　　shoots (cooked strips)
　 1/4 lb. (100 g.) green
　　pepper (strips)
　 1/3 oz. (10 g.) red chili
　　pepper (strips)
④ 1 t. cooking wine
　 1/2 t. each: salt, sesame
　　oil
　 1 t. cornstarch
　 2 T. water
　 2 T. vegetable oil

❶雞肉切絲，加①料醃 10 分鐘。香菇泡軟切絲。

❷油 2 大匙燒熱，下雞肉絲中火炒至變色即刻撈出，餘油續炒香②料，再入③料炒數下，隨入雞肉絲及④料，迅速炒勻即可。

■雞肉可用鴨肉取代。

❶ Cut chicken breast against the grain into strips. Add ① and marinate for 10 minutes.Soak mushrooms in water until soft and cut into strips.

❷ Heat 2 T. oil in preheated wok. Add chicken strips and stir-fry over medium heat until color changes. Remove from heat. In remaining oil, stir-fry ② until fragrant. Add ③ and stir-fry slightly. Add chicken strips and ④; stir-fry until mixed. Remove from heat and serve.

■ Duck may be substituted for chicken.

凉拌果菜絲 APPLE AND BEAN THREAD SALAD

營養含量 Nutritional Content		
蛋白質 Protein	（公克）(g)	5
脂 肪 Fat	（公克）(g)	5
醣 Carbohydrates	（公克）(g)	14
膽固醇 Cholesterol	（毫克）(mg)	14
熱 量 Calories	（大卡）(Cal)	121

1 人份　Per Serving

蘋果（約半個）‥‥‥ 150 公克
（4 兩）
① { 鹽‥‥‥‥‥‥‥‥ ½ 小匙
冷開水‥‥‥‥‥‥‥ 1 杯
粉絲‥ 50 公克（約 1 ½ 兩）
青椒絲‥ 80 公克（約 2 兩）
熟雞絲 60 公克（約 1 ½ 兩）
② { 醬油‥‥‥‥‥‥‥‥ 2 小匙
糖‥‥‥‥‥‥‥‥‥ 1 小匙
白醋‥‥‥‥‥‥‥‥ 1 大匙
麻油‥‥‥‥‥‥‥‥ 2 小匙
蒜末‥‥‥‥‥‥‥‥ 2 小匙
香菜‥‥‥‥‥‥‥‥ 1 大匙

1/3 lb. (150 g.) apple
(about 1/2)
① { 1/2 t. salt
1 c. cold water
1-3/4 oz. (50 g.) bean
threads
2-3/4 oz. (80 g.) green
pepper (strips)
2 oz. (60 g.) chicken
(cooked strips)
② { 2 t. soy sauce
1 t. sugar
1 T. white vinegar
2 t. sesame oil
2 t. garlic (minced)
1 T. coriander

❶蘋果去籽，切絲，泡過①料瀝乾（防止褐變）。粉絲泡軟切約 10 公分長段，入滾水燙熟，取出沖冷開水後備用。

❷所有材料加②料拌勻即可。

❶ Remove apple core and cut unpeeled apple into strips. Rinse in ① and remove to let dry (to prevent browning). Soak bean threads in water until soft and cut into pieces, 4" long. Boil until transparent. Remove with slotted spoon and rinse in cold water. Set aside.

❷ Mix noodles, green pepper strips, apple strips and chicken with ② . Serve.

菠菜牛肉　STIR-FRIED BEEF WITH SPINACH

營養含量 Nutritional Content		
蛋白質 Protein	（公克） (g)	4
脂 肪 Fat	（公克） (g)	12
醣 Carbohydrates	（公克） (g)	3
膽固醇 Cholesterol	（毫克） (mg)	17
熱 量 Calories	（大卡） (Cal)	136

1 人份　Per Serving

牛肉‥‥‥‥ 75 公克（ 2 兩）

① {
沙茶醬‥‥‥‥‥‥‥ 1 大匙
醬油‥‥‥‥‥‥‥‥ ½ 小匙
糖‥‥‥‥‥‥‥‥‥ ½ 小匙
蒜末‥‥‥‥‥‥‥‥ 1 小匙
太白粉‥‥‥‥‥‥‥ 1 小匙
}

菠菜‥200 公克（約 5 ½ 兩）
蔥（ 3 公分長）‥‥‥‥ 6 段
薑絲‥‥‥‥‥‥‥‥‥ 1 大匙
鹽‥‥‥‥‥‥‥‥‥ ⅓ 小匙
沙拉油‥‥‥‥‥‥‥ 2 大匙

2-2/3 oz. (75 g.) beef

① {
1 T. Chinese barbecue
   sauce
1/2 t. soy sauce
1/2 t. sugar
1 t. garlic (minced)
1 t. cornstarch
}

1/2 lb. (200 g.) spinach
6 sections green onion
   (1-1/4")
1 T. shredded ginger
   root
1/3 t. salt
2 T. vegetable oil

❶牛肉橫紋切薄片，加①料醃 10 分鐘，菠菜切 4 公分長段 。

❷油燒熱，將牛肉中火炒至變色即刻取出，餘油爆香蔥薑，再下鹽及菠菜略炒，隨入牛肉迅速炒勻即可。

❶ Cut beef against the grain into thin slices. Add ① and marinate for 10 minutes. Cut spinach into sections, 1-1/2" long.

❷ Heat 2 T. oil in preheated wok. Stir-fry beef over medium heat until color changes. Remove immediately. In remaining oil, quickly stir-fry green onion and ginger until fragrant. Add salt and spinach; stir-fry. Add beef and quickly stir-fry until mixed well. Remove from heat and serve.

鑲洋菇　STUFFED MUSHROOMS

4 人份　Serves 4

營養含量 Nutritional Content		
蛋白質　（公克） Protein　（g）	5
脂　肪　（公克） Fat　（g）	6
醣　　（公克） Carbohydrates　（g）	7
膽固醇　（毫克） Cholesterol　（mg）	13
熱　量　（大卡） Calories　（Cal）	102

1 人份　Per Serving

洋菇(大)………… 200 公克
　　　（約 5 ½ 兩）
絞肉… 60 公克（約 1 ½ 兩）
火腿末…… 15 公克(½ 兩)

① 酒……………………… 1 小匙
鹽……………………… ⅛ 小匙
胡椒………………… ⅛ 小匙
麻油………………… ½ 大匙
太白粉……………… 1 大匙
水…………………… 1 大匙
太白粉……………… 2 大匙

② 高湯………………… 1 杯
鹽…………………… ⅓ 小匙
糖…………………… ¼ 小匙
麻油………………… ½ 大匙
太白粉…………… 1 ½ 小匙

1/2 lb. (200 g.) large button mushrooms
2-1/4 oz. (60 g.) ground pork
1/2 oz. (15 g.) ham (minced)

① 1 t. cooking wine
1/8 t. salt
1/8 t. pepper
1/2 T. sesame oil
1 T. cornstarch
1 T. water
2 T. cornstarch

② 1 c. broth
1/3 t. salt
1/4 t. sugar
1/2 T. sesame oil
1-1/2 t. cornstarch

❶洋菇去蒂，以滾水川燙 30 秒取出。絞肉、火腿末加①料拌勻，備用。
❷洋菇背面(去蒂面)沾上太白粉，鑲上肉餡排於盤上，水開以大火蒸約 5 分鐘取出排盤。
❸將②料煮開淋於洋菇上即可。
■可以燙熟的青江菜圍邊。

❶ Remove stems from button mushrooms. Blanch briefly in boiling water for 30 seconds. Add ① to ground pork and minced ham. Mix evenly and divide into 24 portions.

❷ Dip inner side (where stem was removed) of each button mushroom in cornstarch. Fill each mushroom with meat stuffing and arrange on plate. Place over boiling water and steam over high heat for 5 minutes. Remove from heat and arrange on serving plate.

❸ Bring ② to a boil and pour over stuffed mushrooms. Serve.

■ Boiled bok choy may be arranged around edge of serving plate as garnish.

蘆筍牛肉 ASPARAGUS AND BEEF

營養含量 Nutritional Content		
蛋白質 Protein	（公克）(g)	4
脂肪 Fat	（公克）(g)	10
醣 Carbohydrates	（公克）(g)	2
膽固醇 Cholesterol	（毫克）(mg)	17
熱量 Calories	（大卡）(Cal)	114

1 人份　Per Serving

蘆筍(去老皮)‥‥‥ 140 公克
　　　　　　　（約 4 兩）
洋菇‥ 60 公克(約 1 ½ 兩)
牛肉‥‥‥‥ 75 公克(2 兩)
① ┌ 酒‥‥‥‥‥‥‥‥ 1 小匙
　├ 醬油‥‥‥‥‥‥‥ 1 小匙
　└ 太白粉‥‥‥‥‥‥ 1 小匙
薑絲‥‥ 10 公克(約 ¼ 兩)
② ┌ 酒‥‥‥‥‥‥‥‥ 1 小匙
　├ 鹽‥‥‥‥‥‥‥‥ ½ 小匙
　├ 麻油‥‥‥‥‥‥‥ ½ 小匙
　├ 太白粉‥‥‥‥‥‥ ½ 小匙
　└ 水‥‥‥‥‥‥‥‥ 2 大匙
沙拉油‥‥‥‥‥‥‥‥ 2 大匙

1/3 lb. (140 g.)
　asparagus (peeled)
2-1/4 oz. (60 g.) button
　mushrooms
2-2/3 oz. (75 g.) beef
① ┌ 1 t. cooking wine
　┤ 1 t. soy sauce
　└ 1 t. cornstarch
1/3 oz. (10 g.) shredded
　ginger root
　┌ 1 t. cooking wine
　│ 1/2 t. salt
② ┤ 1/2 t. sesame oil
　│ 1/2 t. cornstarch
　└ 2 T. water
2 T. vegetable oil

❶蘆筍切段(5 公分長)，洋菇切片，牛肉橫紋切薄片，加①料拌勻。

❷油 2 大匙燒熱，入牛肉炒至變色取出，餘油將薑絲爆香，入蘆筍、洋菇炒熟，隨入牛肉及②料炒勻即可。

■可用紅蘿蔔、巴西利彩盤。

❶ Cut asparagus into sections, 2″ long. Slice button mushrooms. Cut beef against the grain into thin strips, add ① and mix.

❷ Heat 2 T. oil in preheated wok. Add beef and stir-fry until color changes. Remove beef. In remaining oil, quickly stir-fry ginger until fragrant. Add asparagus and mushrooms. Stir-fry until done. Add beef and ②; stir-fry until mixed well. Remove from heat and serve.

■ Carrot and parsley may be used as garnish.

銀芽牛肉絲 BEAN SPROUTS AND BEEF STRIPS

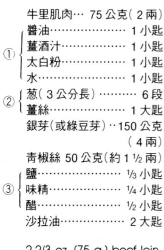

營養含量 Nutritional Content			
蛋白質 Protein	（公克） (g)	4
脂　肪 Fat	（公克） (g)	10
醣 Carbohydrates	（公克） (g)	2
膽固醇 Cholesterol	（毫克） (mg)	17
熱　量 Calories	（大卡） (Cal)	114

1 人份　Per Serving

牛里肌肉… 75 公克（ 2 兩）
① { 醬油……………… 1 小匙
　　薑酒汁…………… 1 小匙
　　太白粉…………… 1 小匙
　　水……………… 1 小匙
② { 葱（ 3 公分長）……… 6 段
　　薑絲……………… 1 大匙
銀芽（或綠豆芽）‥150 公克
　　　　　　　　　（ 4 兩）
青椒絲 50 公克（約 1 ½ 兩）
③ { 鹽……………… ⅓ 小匙
　　味精…………… ¼ 小匙
　　醋……………… ½ 小匙
沙拉油…………… 2 大匙

2-2/3 oz. (75 g.) beef loin
　　(or flank steak)
① { 1 t. soy sauce
　　1 t. ginger wine
　　1 t. cornstarch
　　1 t. water
② { 6 sections green onion
　　(1-1/4")
　　1 T. ginger root (strips)
1/3 lb. (150 g.) mung
　bean sprouts
1-3/4 oz. (50 g.)green
　pepper (strips)
③ { 1/3 t. salt
　　1/2 t. vinegar
　2 T. vegetable oil

❶牛肉橫紋切絲，加①料醃 10 分鐘。

❷油燒熱，入牛肉炒至變色，即刻撈出，餘油爆香②料，入銀芽、青椒絲大火迅速拌炒，並入③料及牛肉炒勻即可。

■銀芽爲綠豆芽摘除頭尾。

■薑酒汁即是用薑拍碎加酒擠出的汁。

❶Cut beef loin against the grain into strips. Add ① and marinate for 10 minutes. Remove ends from mung bean sprouts and set aside.

❷ Heat 2 T. oil in preheated wok. Add beef and stir-fry until color changes. Remove immediately from heat. In remaining oil, quickly stir-fry ② until fragrant. Add mung bean sprouts and green pepper strips; quickly stir-fry over high heat. Add ③ and beef; stir to mix. Remove from heat and serve.

■ To make ginger wine: Add wine to smashed ginger root and then squeeze out liquid.

番茄甜豆牛肉
TOMATOES, PEA PODS, AND BEEF

營養含量 Nutritional Content		
蛋白質 Protein	（公克） (g)	4
脂　肪 Fat	（公克） (g)	10
醣 Carbohydrates	（公克） (g)	3
膽固醇 Cholesterol	（毫克） (mg)	17
熱　量 Calories	（大卡） (Cal)	118

1 人份　Per Serving

牛肉········· 75 公克（2 兩）
① ┌ 酒····················· 1 小匙
　├ 醬油··················· 1 小匙
　└ 太白粉················· 1 小匙
番茄········ 150 公克（4 兩）
葱、薑末·········· 各 1 小匙
甜豆莢(去老筋)··· 50 公克
　　　　　　（約 1½ 兩）
② ┌ 酒····················· 1 小匙
　├ 醬油················· ½ 大匙
　├ 糖····················· 1 小匙
　├ 麻油················· ½ 小匙
　├ 太白粉············· ½ 小匙
　└ 水····················· 2 大匙
沙拉油················ 2 大匙

2-2/3 oz. (75 g.) beef
① ┌ 1 t. cooking wine
　├ 1 t. soy sauce
　└ 1 t. cornstarch
1/3 lb. (150 g.) tomatoes
1 t. green onion
　(minced)
1 t. ginger root
　(minced)
1-3/4 oz. (50 g.) pea
　pods (remove ends
　and strings)
② ┌ 1 t. cooking wine
　├ 1/2 T. soy sauce
　├ 1 t. sugar
　├ 1/2 t. sesame oil
　├ 1/2 t. cornstarch
　└ 2 T. water
2 T. vegetable oil

❶牛肉切薄片，加①料拌勻，番茄切塊備用。

❷油 2 大匙燒熱，下葱薑爆香，入牛肉炒至變色取出，餘油將番茄、甜豆莢炒數下，隨入牛肉及②料炒勻即可。

❶ Thinly slice beef. Add ① and mix evenly. Slice tomatoes and set aside.

❷ Heat 2 T. oil in preheated wok. Add green onion and ginger. Stir-fry until fragrant. Add beef and stir-fry until color changes. Remove from heat. In remaining oil, quickly stir-fry tomatoes and pea pods. Add beef and ②; stir-fry until mixed well. Remove from heat and serve.

四菇鮮湯
CHICKEN WITH ASSORTED MUSHROOMS SOUP

4 人份　Serves 4

營養含量 Nutritional Content		
蛋白質　（公克） Protein　　（g）	6
脂　肪　（公克） Fat　　　（g）	4
醣　　　（公克） Carbohydrates　（g）	4
膽固醇　（毫克） Cholesterol　（mg）	20
熱　量　（大卡） Calories　（Cal）	76

1 人份　Per Serving

香菇····················· 4 朵
雞翅········· 150 公克(4 兩)
金菇　100 公克 (約 2 ½ 兩)
草菇················· 100 公克
洋菇················· 100 公克
① {
水····················· 5 杯
鹽····················· 1 小匙
酒····················· ½ 小匙
薑····················· 3 片
}

4 Chinese black
　mushrooms
1/3 lb. (150 g.) chicken
　wings
1/4 lb. (100 g.) golden
　mushrooms
1/4 lb. (100 g.) straw
　mushrooms
1/4 lb. (100 g.) button
　mushrooms
① {
5 c. water
1 t. salt
1/2 t. cooking wine
3 slices ginger root
}

❶香菇泡軟，雞翅切塊，以滾水川燙 1 分鐘取出備用。
❷將所有材料置蒸碗中，加①料以大火蒸 30 分鐘即可。
■亦可用電鍋(外鍋水 1 杯)蒸熟。
■可以紅蘿蔔花片點綴。

❶ Soak Chinese black mushrooms in water until soft. Chop chicken wings
into pieces. Boil for 1 minute. Remove from heat, drain, and set aside.
❷ Place all ingredients in steaming bowl. Add ① and steam over high heat
for 30 minutes. Serve.
■ Electric rice cooker (1 cup of water in outer pot) may also be used to
steam.
■ Flower-shaped carrot slices may be used as garnish.

銀耳清湯 WHITE FUNGUS SOUP

營養含量 Nutritional Content		
蛋白質 Protein	（公克） (g)	4
脂　肪 Fat	（公克） (g)	3
醣 Carbohydrates	（公克） (g)	3
膽固醇 Cholesterol	（毫克） (mg)	14
熱　量 Calories	（大卡） (Cal)	55

1 人份　Per Serving

白木耳…20 公克（約 ½ 兩）
熟雞肉 60 公克（約 1 ½ 兩）

① 高湯………………… 5 杯
　鹽………………… 1 小匙
　胡椒……………… ⅛ 小匙
　酒………………… 1 小匙
蘿蔔嬰（貝芽菜）…100 公克
　　　　　　　（約 2 ½ 兩）

3/4 oz. (20 g.) white
　fungus
2-1/4 oz. (60 g.) chicken
　meat (cooked)
① 5 c. broth
　1 t. salt
　1/8 t. pepper
　1 t. cooking wine
1/4 lb. (100 g.) white
　radish sprouts

❶白木耳泡軟，雞肉撕成絲。

❷將①料煮開，入白木耳煮滾，改小火煮 30 分鐘，再下雞絲略滾，灑上蘿蔔嬰立即供食。

❶ Soak white fungus in water until soft. Tear chicken meat into strips.

❷ Bring ① to a boil. Add white fungus and bring to a boil. Reduce heat and simmer for 30 minutes. Add chicken strips and boil slightly. When ready to serve, bring to a boil. Sprinkle with white radish sprouts and serve immediately.

酸辣蒟蒻羹 SWEET AND SOUR KONNYAKU SOUP

營養含量 Nutritional Content		
蛋白質 Protein	（公克）(g)	4
脂 肪 Fat	（公克）(g)	3
醣 Carbohydrates	（公克）(g)	4
膽固醇 Cholesterol	（毫克）(mg)	10
熱 量 Calories	（大卡）(Cal)	59

1 人份　Per Serving

① 蒟蒻絲····· 150 公克（4 兩）
　木耳絲··· 30 公克（約 1 兩）
　紅蘿蔔絲 ············30 公克
　里肌肉絲··········· 60 公克
　　　　　　　　（約 1 ½ 兩）

② 醬油················· ½ 小匙
　太白粉··············· 1 小匙
　麻油················· ½ 小匙
　蛋白················· 1 個

③ 水················· 5 杯
　鹽、糖············ 各 1 小匙
　味精················· ¼ 小匙

④ 太白粉··············· 2 大匙
　水··············· 2 大匙

⑤ 醋··············· 2 大匙
　醬油··············· 1 大匙
　胡椒··············· ¼ 小匙
　薑絲、香菜······· 各 1 大匙

① 1/3 lb. (150 g.) konnyaku
　1 oz. (30 g.) wood ears (strips)
　1 oz. (30 g.) carrots (strips)
　2 oz. (60 g.) pork loin (strips)

② 1/2 t. soy sauce
　1 t. cornstarch
　1/2 t. sesame oil
　1 egg white

③ 5 c. water
　1 t. each: salt, sugar

④ 2 T. cornstarch } mix
　2 T. water

⑤ 2 T. vinegar
　1 T. soy sauce
　1/4 t. black pepper
　1 T. shredded ginger root
　1 T. coriander

❶①料川燙片刻取出，里肌肉絲加②料拌勻，蛋白打勻備用。

❷將③料煮開，下①料待滾，加入肉絲，以④料勾芡，再將打勻的蛋白徐徐加入後熄火，隨即拌入⑤料，並 撒上薑絲、香菜即成。

❶ Briefly blanch ① in boiling water and remove from heat. Mix pork strips with②. Beat egg white evenly. Set aside.

❷ Bring ③ to a boil. Add ① and bring to another boil. Add pork strips. Thicken with ④. Remove from heat. Add⑤. Sprinkle with ginger and coriander. Serve.

排骨海帶蘿蔔湯
PORK RIBS, SEAWEED, AND TURNIP SOUP

營養含量 Nutritional Content		
蛋白質 Protein	（公克）(g)	5
脂肪 Fat	（公克）(g)	3
醣 Carbohydrates	（公克）(g)	4
膽固醇 Cholesterol	（毫克）(mg)	13
熱量 Calories	（大卡）(Cal)	63

1 人份　Per Serving

小排骨…………… 100 公克
　　　　　　（約 2 ½ 兩）
紅蘿蔔… 70 公克(約 2 兩)
白蘿蔔…………… 200 公克
　　　　　　（約 5 ½ 兩）
海帶結 50 公克(約 1 ½ 兩)
水………………… 7 杯
薑………………… 3 片
鹽………………… 1 小匙

3-1/2 oz. (100 g.) pork
　ribs
2-1/2 oz. (70 g.) carrots
1/2 lb. (200 g.) Chinese
　turnip
1-3/4 oz. (50 g.)
　seaweed knots
7 c. water
3 slices ginger root
1 t. salt

❶小排骨切 3 公分塊狀，以滾水川燙 30 秒取出，紅、白蘿蔔切（ 4×2×2 公分）塊狀。

❷水煮開，加入所有材料及薑片以大火煮滾，改小火燜煮 30 分鐘，加鹽調味即可。

❶ Cut spareribs into 1-1/4" pieces; blanch in boiling water for 30 seconds and remove from heat. Dice carrots and turnips into 1-1/2" x 3/4" pieces.

❷ Bring water to a boil. Add all ingredients and ginger slices. Bring to another boil. Reduce heat and simmer for 30 minutes. Season with salt to taste. Serve.

雪花牛肉羹 EGG WHITE BEEF AND SPINACH SOUP

營養含量 Nutritional Content		
蛋白質 Protein	（公克）(g)	5
脂　肪 Fat	（公克）(g)	3
醣 Carbohydrates	（公克）(g)	4
膽固醇 Cholesterol	（毫克）(mg)	17
熱　量 Calories	（大卡）(Cal)	63

1 人份　Per Serving

牛肉(里肌肉)‥‥‥ 75 公克
　　　　　　　　（2 兩）
① 鹽‥‥‥‥‥‥‥‥ ⅛ 小匙
　 太白粉‥‥‥‥‥‥ 1 小匙
菠菜‥100 公克（約 2 ½ 兩）
蛋白‥‥‥‥‥‥‥‥ 1 個
　 水‥‥‥‥‥‥‥‥ 5 杯
② 鹽‥‥‥‥‥‥‥‥ 1 小匙
　 胡椒‥‥‥‥‥‥‥ ⅛ 小匙
③ 太白粉‥‥‥‥‥‥ 2 大匙
　 水‥‥‥‥‥‥‥‥ 2 大匙
火腿末‥‥‥‥‥‥‥ 1 小匙

2-2/3 oz. (75 g.) beef loin
　(or flank steak)
① 1/8 t. salt
　 1 t. cornstarch
　 1/4 lb. (100 g.) spinach
　 1 egg white
② 5 c. water
　 1 t. salt
　 1/8 t. pepper
③ 2 T. cornstarch　} mix
　 2 T. water
　 1 t. ham (minced)

❶牛肉逆紋切 1 公分正方薄片，加①料拌勻，菠菜燙軟切碎，蛋白以打蛋器順同方向打至呈雪花泡沫。

❷②料煮開，入牛肉、菠菜，並以③料勾芡，加入蛋白泡沫煮開，置湯碗中，撒上火腿末即可。

■牛肉可改用豬肉代替。

❶ Cut beef against the grain into thin slices, 1/2″ x 1/2″. Add ① and mix evenly. Blanch and chop spinach. Beat egg whites consistently in one direction until white and fluffy.

❷ Bring ② to a boil. Add beef and spinach. Thicken with ③. Add beaten egg whites to beef mixture and bring to a boil. Pour into soup bowl, sprinkle with minced ham and serve.

■ Pork may be substituted for beef.

海產類　SEAFOOD

1. 降低血中脂質的魚類油脂

在經濟蓬勃發展的國家，心血管性疾病在死亡原因排行榜上經常是獨占鰲頭，嚴重威脅人們的生命安全。而終年以魚肉類爲主食的愛斯基摩人卻極少罹患此類疾病，原來魚類（尤其是深海魚類）含有一種不飽和脂肪，可以清除血管壁上堆積的脂質，具有清道夫的作用，爲動植物所無。

魚類脂肪，不僅能降低血中的膽固醇及其他的脂質，預防心血管方面的疾病，還能加強人體免疫系統，降低發炎症的發生率等。對於不常食用者而言，每週若能擇取一至二次，定能有所助益。

2. 享受蝦蟹口福又何妨

魚貝類也是良好的蛋白質來源，其脂肪含量雖較其他肉類爲低，而其膽固醇含量卻比肉類高。但魚貝類的不飽和脂肪酸也比較高，有降低血中膽固醇的功能，因此，魚貝類不僅不需要承擔心血管疾病的罪名，還可說是功臣呢！即使有動脈硬化傾向的家屬，無須特意規避，只要不吃腦、魚卵及內臟，而且各類食物搭配適宜，享受蝦蟹口福又何妨！

1. FISH FATS—REDUCE FAT IN THE BLOOD

In economically prosperous countries, cardiovascular diseases are normally ranked as one of the top causes of death. Yet Eskimos, who have a diet mainly composed of fish and meat, enjoy the lowest incidence of these diseases. Fish (especially deep sea fish), unlike other animals and plants, contain a type of unsaturated fat which can expel fats accumulated on blood vessel walls.

Fish fats are not only able to reduce cholesterol and other fats in the blood but can also prevent cardiovascular diseases. Fish fats are also able to strengthen the immune system and reduce the occurrence of infections. For those who don't consume fish on a regular basis, eating fish once or twice a week can be highly beneficial.

2. ENJOYING THE DELICIOUS FLAVOR AND HARMLESSNESS OF SHRIMP AND CRAB

Shellfish are also a fine source of protein. Although their fat content is lower than that of other meats, their cholesterol level is higher. But the amount of unsaturated fatty acids in shellfish is higher and serves to reduce blood cholesterol. Therefore, shellfish consumers need not worry about contracting cardiovascular diseases, for shellfish can even serve to guard against such illnesses. Those families in which there is a high incidence of 'hardening of the arteries' don't need to particularly avoid eating shellfish as long as the brain, eggs, and internal organs are not consumed. Furthermore, the proper coordination of other foods enables one to freely enjoy the delicious flavor of shrimps and crabs without risking health dangers.

烤油帶

BAKED RIBBONFISH

營養含量 Nutritional Content		
蛋白質 Protein	（公克）(g)	13
脂 肪 Fat	（公克）(g)	9
醣 Carbohydrates	（公克）(g)	1
膽固醇 Cholesterol	（毫克）(mg)	36
熱 量 Calories	（大卡）(Cal)	133

1 人份　Per Serving

帶魚⋯⋯ 300 公克（8 兩）

① 薑酒汁⋯⋯⋯⋯⋯ 1 小匙
鹽⋯⋯⋯⋯⋯⋯ ½ 小匙
胡椒粉⋯⋯⋯⋯⋯ ⅛ 小匙
檸檬⋯⋯⋯⋯⋯⋯ 半個

2/3 lb. (300 g.) ribbonfish

① 1 t. ginger wine
1/2 t. salt
1/8 t. pepper
1/2 lemon

❶魚兩面切交叉花紋，擦乾水份，抹上①料，醃 15 分鐘，置烤盤中。

❷烤箱燒熱至 400℉ ，將魚烤熟（約 15 分鐘）取出，食時淋上檸檬汁即可。

■可以生荣葉、檸檬等彩盤。

❶ Cut crisscross slits on both sides of fish. Dry and rub with ①. Let stand for 15 minutes. Place directly in baking pan.

❷ Pre-heat oven to 400 degrees and bake fish for approximately 15 minutes. Remove and place on serving dish. Squeeze lemon juice over fish and serve.

■ Lettuce and lemon slices may be used as garnish.

川草魚　BOILED FISH

營養含量 Nutritional Content		
蛋白質　（公克） Protein　　（g）		11
脂　肪　（公克） Fat　　　（g）		11
醣　　　（公克） Carbohydrates（g）		1
膽固醇　（毫克） Cholesterol　（mg）		30
熱　量　（大卡） Calories　（Cal）		143

1 人份　Per Serving

活草魚（或鯰魚）300 公克
　　　　　　　　（ 8 兩 ）

①
水‧‧‧‧‧‧‧‧‧‧‧‧‧‧‧‧‧ 10 杯
葱（ 3 公分長 ）‧‧‧‧‧‧ 2 段
薑‧‧‧‧‧‧‧‧‧‧‧‧‧‧‧‧‧‧ 3 片
酒‧‧‧‧‧‧‧‧‧‧‧‧‧‧‧‧ 1 大匙
鹽‧‧‧‧‧‧‧‧‧‧‧‧‧‧‧‧ 1 小匙

②
葱絲、薑絲‧‧‧‧‧‧ 各 1 大匙
紅辣椒絲‧‧‧‧‧‧‧‧‧‧ 1 大匙

③
煮魚汁‧‧‧‧‧‧‧‧‧‧‧‧‧‧ 1 杯
醬油‧‧‧‧‧‧‧‧‧‧‧‧‧‧ 1 大匙
糖‧‧‧‧‧‧‧‧‧‧‧‧‧‧‧‧ ½ 小匙

④
太白粉‧‧‧‧‧‧‧‧‧‧‧‧‧‧ 1 小匙
水‧‧‧‧‧‧‧‧‧‧‧‧‧‧‧‧ 1 大匙

香菜‧‧‧‧‧‧‧‧‧‧‧‧‧‧‧‧ 2 大匙
嫩薑絲‧‧‧‧‧‧‧‧‧‧‧‧‧‧ 2 大匙
沙拉油‧‧‧‧‧‧‧‧‧‧‧‧‧‧ 1 大匙

2/3 lb. (300 g.) grass
　carp (or catfish)

①
10 c. water
2 sections green onions
3 slices ginger root
1 T. cooking wine
1 t. salt

②
1 T. shredded green
　onion
1 T. shredded ginger
　root
1 T. shredded red chili
　pepper

③
1 c. fish stock
1 T. soy sauce
1/2 t. sugar

④
1 t. cornstarch
1 T. water
} mix

2 T. coriander
2 T. shredded baby
　ginger root
1 T. vegetable oil

❶將①料煮滾，入草魚大火煮滾 1 分鐘，即刻關火燜 5 分鐘至魚肉熟，取出置盤上。煮魚之湯汁留 1 杯備用。

❷油燒熱，下②料炒香，隨入③料煮滾，再以④料勾芡，淋於魚上，撒上香菜，嫩薑即可。

❶ Bring ① to a boil. Add grass carp and boil over high heat for 1 minute. Turn off heat, cover, and let stand for 5 minutes until carp is done. Remove and place on plate. Reserve 1 cup of fish stock for ③。

❷ Heat 1 T. oil. in preheated wok. Stir-fry ② until fragrant. Add ③ and bring to a boil. Thicken with ④ and pour over fish. Sprinkle with coriander and baby ginger root. Serve.

■Ginger root may be substituted for baby ginger root.

鍋塌鱈魚　PEKING-STYLE FRIED FISH

4 人份　Serves 4

營養含量 Nutritional Content		
蛋白質 Protein	（公克） (g)	10
脂　肪 Fat	（公克） (g)	13
醣 Carbohydrates	（公克） (g)	2
膽固醇 Cholesterol	（毫克） (mg)	51
熱　量 Calories	（大卡） (Cal)	165

1 人份　Per Serving

鱈魚‥210 公克（約 5 ½ 兩）
①｛ 鹽‥‥‥‥‥‥‥‥‥ ¼ 小匙
　　 酒‥‥‥‥‥‥‥‥‥ ½ 小匙
麵粉‥‥‥‥‥‥‥ 1 ½ 大匙
蛋‥‥‥‥‥‥‥‥‥ ½ 個
葱末‥‥‥‥‥‥‥‥ 2 小匙
薑末‥‥‥‥‥‥‥‥ 2 小匙
②｛ 酒‥‥‥‥‥‥‥‥‥ ½ 小匙
　　 鹽‥‥‥‥‥‥‥‥‥ ½ 小匙
　　 麻油‥‥‥‥‥‥‥‥ ½ 小匙
　　 高湯‥‥‥‥‥‥‥‥ 3 大匙
檸檬‥‥‥‥‥‥‥‥‥ 2 片
沙拉油‥‥‥‥‥‥‥ 1 ½ 大匙

① ｛ 1/2 lb. (210 g.) cod
　　 1/4 t. salt
　　 1/2 t. cooking wine
1-1/2 T. flour
1/2 egg
2 t. green onion
　(minced)
2 t. ginger root
　(minced)
② ｛ 1/2 t. cooking wine
　　 1/2 t. salt
　　 1/2 t. sesame oil
　　 3 T. broth
2 slices lemon
1-1/2 T. vegetable oil

❶鱈魚切 1.5 公分厚片，抹上①料醃 10 分鐘，沾上麵粉，再沾上打勻之蛋液。

❷油燒熱，將魚片入鍋，中火煎至兩面呈金黃色（約 2 分鐘），洒上葱、薑末及②料，用叉子或牙籤叉透魚肉使之入味，改小火塌至汁乾即可。

■可以番茄、巴西利、櫻桃彩盤。

❶ Cut fish meat into 2/3'' thick slices. Marinate fish in ① for 10 minutes. Dip fish in flour and then in well-beaten egg.

❷ Heat 1-1/2 T. oil in preheated wok. Add fish slices and fry over medium heat until both sides are golden (about 2 minutes). Sprinkle minced green onions, minced ginger, and ② over fish. Make punctures in fish with fork or toothpick to allow flavor to seep in. Reduce heat and cook until juice is almost absorbed. Sprinkle lemon juice on fish before serving.

■Tomatoes, parsley, and cherries may be used as garnish.

椒鹽鯧魚　SALT AND PEPPER POMFRET

4 人份　Serves 4

營養含量 Nutritional Content		
蛋白質　（公克） Protein　（g）		10
脂　肪　（公克） Fat　（g）		14
醣　　（公克） Carbohydrates　（g）		—
膽固醇　（毫克） Cholesterol　（mg）		28
熱　量　（大卡） Calories　（Cal）		166

1 人份　Per Serving

白鯧魚············ 280 公克
　　　　　　（約 7 ½ 兩）
① ⎧ 葱 (3 公分長)········· 2 段
　 ⎪ 薑·············· 3 片
　 ⎨ 鹽·············· ¼ 小匙
　 ⎩ 酒·············· 1 小匙
② ⎧ 花椒粉············· ⅛ 小匙
　 ⎩ 鹽·············· ¼ 小匙
　　 葱花············· 1 大匙
　　 沙拉油············ 3 杯

2/3 lb. (280 g.) white
　　pomfret
① ⎧ 2 sections green onion
　 ⎪ 3 slices ginger root
　 ⎨ 1/4 t. salt
　 ⎩ 1 t. cooking wine
② ⎧ 1/8 t. Szechuan
　 ⎪ 　peppercorn powder
　 ⎩ 1/4 t. salt
　　 1 T. green onion
　　　(chopped)
　　 3 c. vegetable oil

❶鯧魚兩面切交叉花紋，抹上①料醃 10 分鐘。

❷油燒熱，入魚炸至兩面呈金黃色（約 5 分鐘），取出置盤上，撒上葱花及②料即可。

■魚亦可用油煎熟。

■可以番茄、生菜、紅辣椒等彩盤。

❶ Cut criss-cross slashes on both sides of pomfret. Add ① and marinate for 10 minutes.

❷ Heat 3 c. oil in preheated wok. Add fish and deep-fry until both sides are golden (about 5 minutes). Remove fish and arrange on serving plate. Sprinkle with chopped green onion and ②. Serve.

■ Fish may be stir-fried instead of deep-fried.

■ Tomatoes, lettuce, and red chili peppers may be used as garnish.

香醋烹魚　FISH IN VINEGAR SAUCE

4 人份　Serves 4

營養含量 Nutritional Content		
蛋白質 Protein	（公克） (g)	11
脂　肪 Fat	（公克） (g)	12
醣 Carbohydrates	（公克） (g)	—
膽固醇 Cholesterol	（毫克） (mg)	32
熱　量 Calories	（大卡） (Cal)	152

1 人份　Per Serving

魚···· 250 公克（約 6 ½ 兩）
①
鹽·················· ¼ 小匙
薑酒汁··············· 2 小匙
太白粉··············· 1 大匙
②
黑醋················· 1 大匙
醬油················· 1 大匙
糖·················· ½ 小匙
麻油················· ½ 小匙
③
葱絲················· 2 大匙
薑絲················· 1 大匙
紅辣椒絲············· 1 小匙
沙拉油··············· 1 大匙

1/2 lb. (250 g.) fish
①
1/4 t. salt
2 t. ginger wine
1 T. cornstarch
②
1 T. black vinegar
1 T. soy sauce
1/2 t. sugar
1/2 t. sesame oil
③
2 T. shredded green
onion
1 T. shredded ginger
root
1 t. shredded red chili
peppers
1 T. vegetable oil

❶魚切 1.5 公分厚之片狀，以①料醃 10 分鐘。

❷油燒熱，入魚煎熟並至兩面呈金黃色（約 3 分鐘），隨入②料即刻取出盛盤上，撒上③料即成。

■可以香菜、小紅蘿蔔彩盤。

❶ Slice fish into pieces, 2/3″ thick. Marinate in ① for 10 minutes.
❷ Heat 1 T. oil in preheated wok. Add fish and fry until both sides are golden (about 3 minutes). Add ② and remove immediately. Arrange on serving plate. Sprinkle with ③ and serve.
■Coriander and small carrots may be used as garnish.

粟米石斑魚 STIR-FRIED ROCK COD

營養含量 Nutritional Content		
蛋白質 Protein	（公克） (g)	9
脂　肪 Fat	（公克） (g)	13
醣 Carbohydrates	（公克） (g)	2
膽固醇 Cholesterol	（毫克） (mg)	26
熱　量 Calories	（大卡） (Cal)	161

1 人份　Per Serving

石斑魚肉‥‥‥‥ 200 公克
　　　　　　（約 5½ 兩）
① ⎰鹽‥‥‥‥‥‥‥‥ ¼ 小匙
　⎱薑酒汁‥‥‥‥‥‥ 1 小匙
　⎰太白粉‥‥‥‥‥‥ 2 小匙
② ⎰玉米醬‥‥‥‥‥‥ 4 大匙
　⎱雞蛋白‥‥‥‥‥‥ ½ 個
　蔥（3 公分長）‥‥‥ 3 段
　⎛高湯‥‥‥‥‥‥‥ ¼ 杯
　⎜糖‥‥‥‥‥‥‥‥ ½ 小匙
③ ⎨麻油‥‥‥‥‥‥‥ ½ 小匙
　⎜太白粉‥‥‥‥‥‥ ½ 小匙
　⎝鹽‥‥‥‥‥‥‥‥ ¼ 小匙
　蔥花‥‥‥‥‥‥‥ 1 大匙
　沙拉油‥‥‥‥‥‥ 5 大匙

1/2 lb. (200 g.) rock cod
　or other white fish
　meat
① ⎰1/4 t. salt
　⎨1 t. ginger wine
　⎱2 t. cornstarch
② ⎰4 T. creamed corn
　⎨　(canned)
　⎱1/2 egg white
　3 sections green onion
　　(1-1/4″)
　⎛1/4 c. broth
　⎜1/2 t. sugar
③ ⎨1/2 t. sesame oil
　⎜1/2 t. cornstarch
　⎝1/4 t. salt
　1 T. green onion
　　(chopped)
　5 T. vegetable oil

❶魚肉表面切交叉花紋，再切成 4×4×1 公分之塊狀，加①料醃 10 分鐘，②料調勻備用。

❷油燒熱，入魚肉炒至變色並熟取出排盤上，留油 1 大匙將蔥段爆香，入③料煮滾，加入調勻之②料煮開，淋於魚上，撒上蔥花即可。

■可以香菜、小紅蘿蔔彩盤。

❶ Cut crisscross slashes on surface of fish meat and cut into 1-1/2″ x 1-1/2″ x 1/2″ pieces. Add ① and marinate for 10 minutes. Mix ② and set aside.

❷ Heat 5 T. oil in preheated wok. Add fish and stir-fry until color changes. Remove from heat when done and arrange on serving plate. Leave 1 T. oil in wok. Stir-fry green onion sections until fragrant. Add ③ and bring to a boil. Add evenly-mixed ② and bring to another boil. Remove from heat. Pour over fish. Sprinkle with chopped green onion and serve.

■Coriander and carrot may be used as garnish.

蒜香燒魚　GARLIC FLAVORED FISH

營養含量 Nutritional Content		
蛋白質 Protein	（公克） (g)	9
脂　肪 Fat	（公克） (g)	14
醣 Carbohydrates	（公克） (g)	1
膽固醇 Cholesterol	（毫克） (mg)	26
熱　量 Calories	（大卡） (Cal)	166

1 人份　Per Serving

魚(取中段或魚片)　210公克
　　　　　　　　　　　(約5 ½兩)

① { 薑酒汁……………… 1 小匙
　　鹽………………… ¼ 小匙

② { 蒜頭(去皮)……… 12 粒
　　薑………………… 3 片
　　葱(3 公分長)……… 3 段

③ { 酒………………… ½ 大匙
　　醬油……………… 1 大匙
　　黑醋……………… ½ 大匙
　　糖………………… 1 小匙
　　水………………… 1 杯

④ { 太白粉…………… 1 小匙
　　水………………… 1 大匙
　　沙拉油…………… 2 大匙

1/2 lb. (210 g.) fish
　(middle section or
　fish slices)

① { 1 t. ginger wine
　　1/4 t. salt

② { 12 cloves garlic
　　　(peeled)
　　3 slices ginger root
　　3 sections green onion
　　　(1-1/4″)

　　2 T. vegetable oil

③ { 1/2 T. cooking wine
　　1 T. soy sauce
　　1/2 T. black vinegar
　　1 t. sugar
　　1 c. water

④ { 1 t. cornstarch   } mix
　　1 T. water

　　2 T. vegetable oil

❶魚抹上①料醃 15 分鐘。

❷油燒熱，魚入鍋將兩面煎黃取出，餘油炒香②料，再下魚及③料煮開，改小火燜煮 5 分鐘，將魚鏟出置盤上，餘汁以④料勾芡，淋於魚上即成。

■可以紅蘿蔔、生菜、香荽等彩盤。

❶ Marinate fish in ① for 15 minutes.

❷ Heat 2 T. oil in preheated wok.Add fish and fry until both sides are golden; remove from heat. In remaining oil, stir-fry ② until fragrant. Add fish and③. Bring to a boil. Reduce heat and simmer for 5 minutes. Remove fish with slotted spoon and arrange on serving plate. Thicken remaining juices with④. Pour over fish and serve.

■Carrots, lettuce, and coriander may be used as garnish.

清蒸魚

STEAMED FISH

營養含量 Nutritional Content		
蛋白質 Protein	（公克） (g)	13
脂　肪 Fat	（公克） (g)	10
醣 Carbohydrates	（公克） (g)	—
膽固醇 Cholesterol	（毫克） (mg)	38
熱　量 Calories	（大卡） (Cal)	142

1 人份　Per Serving

鯧魚或鱈魚300 公克(8 兩)
① 鹽…………………… ½ 小匙
　 酒…………………… 1 小匙
　 醬油………………… ½ 小匙
② 香菇絲……………… 1 大匙
　 薑絲………………… 1 大匙
③ 胡椒………………… ⅛ 小匙
　 麻油………………… ½ 小匙
④ 葱絲………………… ½ 杯
　 薑絲………………… 1 大匙

2/3 lb. (300 g.) pomfret, cod (or any fish with few bones)
① 1/2 t. salt
　 1 t. cooking wine
　 1/2 t. soy sauce
② 1 T. shredded Chinese black mushroom
　 1 T. shredded ginger root
③ 1/8 t. pepper
　 1/2 t. sesame oil
④ 1/2 c. shredded green onion
　 1 T. shredded ginger root

❶將魚切 1.5 公分厚之片狀，盛盤上加①料醃 10 分鐘後，擺上②料，水開以大火蒸熟(約 8 分鐘)，取出撒上③料及④料即可。

■可以紅蘿蔔、香菜彩盤。

❶ Cut fish into slices, ⅔" thick. Place on dish, add ① and marinate for 10 minutes. Sprinkle ② over fish. Place fish over boiling water and steam over high heat for about 8 minutes or until done. Remove from heat. Sprinkle with ③ and ④ . Serve.

■ Carrots and coriander may be used as garnish.

瓜薑魚絲　FISH AND PICKLED CUCUMBER STRIPS

4 人份　Serves 4

營養含量 Nutritional Content		
蛋白質 Protein	（公克） (g)	9
脂　肪 Fat	（公克） (g)	13
醣 Carbohydrates	（公克） (g)	—
膽固醇 Cholesterol	（毫克） (mg)	26
熱　量 Calories	（大卡） (Cal)	153

1 人份　Per Serving

魚肉‥200 公克（約 5 ½ 兩）

①
酒⋯⋯⋯⋯⋯⋯⋯ 2 小匙
鹽⋯⋯⋯⋯⋯⋯⋯ ¼ 小匙
麻油⋯⋯⋯⋯⋯⋯ ½ 小匙
太白粉⋯⋯⋯⋯⋯ 1 大匙

醬瓜⋯ 50 公克（約 1 ½ 兩）
葱絲⋯⋯⋯⋯⋯⋯ 2 大匙
嫩薑絲⋯⋯⋯⋯⋯ 3 大匙
沙拉油⋯⋯⋯⋯⋯ 5 大匙

1/2 lb. (200 g.) fish meat

①
2 t. cooking wine
1/4 t. salt
1/2 t. sesame oil
1 T. cornstarch

1-3/4 oz. (50 g.)
　pickled cucumbers
2 T. shredded green
　onion
3 T. shredded baby
　ginger root
5 T. vegetable oil

❶魚肉切粗絲，加①料拌勻，醬瓜切絲備用。

❷油燒熱，入魚肉炒至變色取出，留油 1 大匙將葱、薑炒香，隨入醬瓜、魚肉拌勻即可。

■可以小黃瓜圍邊。

❶ Slice fish meat into thick strips. Add ① and mix. Slice cucumbers and set aside.

❷ Heat 5 T. oil in preheated wok. Add fish and stir-fry until golden. Remove from heat. Leave 1 T. oil in wok. Stir-fry green onion and ginger until fragrant. Add cucumbers and fish; stir until mixed well. Remove from heat and serve.

■Gherkin cucumbers may be arranged around edge of serving plate as garnish.

■Ginger root may be substituted for baby ginger root.

炒蟹腿　STIR-FRIED CRAB LEGS

4 人份　Serves 4

營養含量 Nutritional Content		
蛋白質 Protein	（公克） (g)	11
脂　肪 Fat	（公克） (g)	26
醣 Carbohydrates	（公克） (g)	0
膽固醇 Cholesterol	（毫克） (mg)	48
熱　量 Calories	（大卡） (Cal)	278

1 人份　Per Serving

蟹腿⋯⋯ 330 公克(約 9 兩)
薑酒汁⋯⋯⋯⋯⋯ 2 小匙
①{ 紅辣椒⋯⋯⋯⋯⋯ 1 大匙
　 葱花⋯⋯⋯⋯⋯⋯ 2 大匙
　 蒜末⋯⋯⋯⋯⋯⋯ 2 小匙
②{ 醬油膏(或醬油)⋯⋯ 2 大匙
　 酒⋯⋯⋯⋯⋯⋯⋯ 1 小匙
　 糖⋯⋯⋯⋯⋯⋯ ½ 小匙
　 黑醋⋯⋯⋯⋯⋯⋯ 1 大匙
　 水⋯⋯⋯⋯⋯⋯⋯ ½ 杯
葱花或九層塔⋯⋯⋯ 2 大匙
沙拉油⋯⋯⋯⋯⋯⋯ 2 大匙

3/4 lb (330 g.) crab legs
2 t. ginger wine
① { 1 T. red pepper
　 2 T. green onion
　 (chopped)
　 2 t. garlic (minced)
② { 2 T. soy sauce paste or
　 soy sauce
　 1 t. cooking wine
　 1/2 t. sugar
　 1 T. black vinegar
　 1/2 c. water
2 T. green onion
(chopped) or fresh
basil leaves
2 T. vegetable oil

❶蟹腿稍拍，以薑酒汁醃 10 分鐘。

❷油燒熱，將①料炒香，入蟹腿炒數下，隨入②料大火煮滾，改小火燜煮 5 分鐘，入葱花拌勻即可。

■蟹腿可改用蟹塊。

❶ Slightly pound crab legs (to break shell so that meat may be easily extracted when eating). Marinate in ginger wine for 10 minutes.

❷ Heat 2 T. oil in preheated wok. Stir-fry ① until fragrant. Add crab legs and quickly stir-fry. Add ② and bring to a boil. Reduce heat and simmer for 5 minutes. Add chopped green onion; stir to mix. Remove from heat and serve.

■ Crab pieces may be substituted for crab legs. If large crab legs are used, cut them into pieces before marinating.

生菜魚鬆
LETTUCE-WRAPPED SHREDDED FISH

4 人份　Serves 4

營養含量 Nutritional Content		
蛋白質 Protein	（公克） (g)	8
脂　肪 Fat	（公克） (g)	13
醣 Carbohydrates	（公克） (g)	3
膽固醇 Cholesterol	（毫克） (mg)	52
熱　量 Calories	（大卡） (Cal)	161

1 人份　Per Serving

魚肉‥125 公克（約 2 ½ 兩）
蝦仁……… 30 公克（約 1 兩）
① 薑酒汁…………………… 1 小匙
　 蛋黃…………………………… 1 個
② 香菇………………………… 2 朵
　 洋葱、芹菜、熟筍 各30公克
炸米粉…20 公克（約 ½ 兩）
③ 鹽、糖………… 各 ½ 小匙
　 醬油…………………… 1 小匙
　 麻油…………………… ½ 小匙
　 太白粉………………… ½ 小匙
　 水………………………… 2 小匙
熟青豆仁………… 30 公克
生菜葉…………… 12 葉
沙拉油…………… 2 大匙

1/4 lb. (125 g.) fish meat
1 oz. (30 g.) shrimp
　(shelled)
① { 1 t. ginger wine
　　1 egg yolk
② { 2 Chinese black
　　　mushrooms
　　1 oz. (30 g.) onion
　　1 oz. (30 g.) celery
　　1 oz. (30 g.) bamboo
　　　shoots (cooked)
3/4 oz. (20 g.) fried rice
　noodles
③ { 1/2 t. salt
　　1/2 t. sugar
　　1 t. soy sauce
　　1/2 t. sesame oil
　　1/2 t. cornstarch
　　2 t. water
1 oz. (30 g.) green peas
　(cooked)
12 leaves lettuce
2 T. vegetable oil

❶魚肉、蝦仁切碎，加①料拌勻，②料亦切碎，炸米粉鋪盤。

❷油燒熱，入調好之魚肉、蝦仁等炒至變色鏟出，隨入香菇、洋葱炒香，再下筍及芹菜略炒，並下魚肉等迅速拌勻，最後加入③料及青豆仁，炒勻即可盛起置炸米粉上。

❸食時以生菜包食即可。

■炸米粉方法：油燒至十分熱，下乾米粉炸至金黃色即刻取出。

❶ Finely chop fish meat and shrimp. Add ① and mix evenly. Finely chop ②. Arrange fried rice noodles on serving plate.

❷ Heat 2 T. oil in preheated wok .Add already mixed fish meat and shrimp. Stir-fry until color changes; remove from heat. Stir-fry mushrooms and onions until fragrant. Add bamboo shoots and celery. Quickly blend in fish /shrimp mixture. Add ③ and green peas; stir-fry until mixed well. Pour over fried rice noodles.

❸ Fish/shrimp mixture is served by wrapping in lettuce leaves.

■ To fry rice noodles: Heat oil until hot. Add dried rice noodles. Fry until golden and immediately remove from heat.

洋葱魚肉餅 ONION FISH CAKES

營養含量 Nutritional Content		
蛋白質 Protein	（公克） (g)	9
脂　肪 Fat	（公克） (g)	12
醣 Carbohydrates	（公克） (g)	4
膽固醇 Cholesterol	（毫克） (mg)	22
熱　量 Calories	（大卡） (Cal)	160

1 人份　Per Serving

鯕魚肉⋯⋯⋯⋯⋯ 170 公克
（或鯊魚肉，約 4 ½ 兩）
洋葱⋯ 90 公克（約 2 ½ 兩）

①
酒⋯⋯⋯⋯⋯⋯⋯ ½ 大匙
鹽⋯⋯⋯⋯⋯⋯⋯ ¼ 小匙
糖⋯⋯⋯⋯⋯⋯⋯ ½ 小匙
醬油⋯⋯⋯⋯⋯⋯ 2 小匙
麻油⋯⋯⋯⋯⋯⋯ 1 小匙
蛋白⋯⋯⋯⋯⋯⋯ 1 個
太白粉⋯⋯⋯⋯⋯ 2 大匙

②
醬油⋯⋯⋯⋯⋯⋯ ½ 大匙
黑醋⋯⋯⋯⋯⋯⋯ 1 小匙
糖⋯⋯⋯⋯⋯⋯⋯ ½ 小匙
沙拉油⋯⋯⋯⋯⋯ 1 ½ 大匙

1/3 lb. (170 g.) spear fish
　　meat (or shark meat)
3-1/4 oz. (90 g.) onion

①
1/2 T. cooking wine
1/4 t. salt
1/2 t. sugar
2 t. soy sauce
1 t. sesame oil
1 egg white
2 T. cornstarch

②
1/2 T. soy sauce
1 t. black vinegar
1/2 t. sugar
1-1/2 T. vegetable oil

❶魚肉剁成泥，洋葱切碎同置盆中，加①料拌勻，分成 8 等份，每份分別壓扁成魚肉餅。

❷油燒熱，以小火將魚肉餅煎熟並呈金黃色（約 4 分鐘），隨入②料即刻取出盛盤。

■可以茄子、櫻桃等彩盤。

❶ Mash fish meat. Finely chop onion. Place both in bowl. Add ① and mix well. Divide fish mixture into 8 portions and then press flat to make 8 fish cakes.

❷ Heat 1-1/2 T. oil in preheated wok and fry fish cakes over low heat until golden (about 4 minutes). Add ② and remove immediately. Serve.

■ Eggplant, cherries, etc. may be used as garnish.

雙筍魚捲
FISH, ASPARAGUS, AND BAMBOO SHOOT ROLLS

4 人份　Serves 4

營養含量 Nutritional Content		
蛋白質 Protein	（公克） (g)	11
脂　肪 Fat	（公克） (g)	9
醣 Carbohydrates	（公克） (g)	3
膽固醇 Cholesterol	（毫克） (mg)	30
熱　量 Calories	（大卡） (Cal)	137

1 人份　Per Serving

　　魚肉……… 225 公克（6 兩）
　①{ 鹽………………………… ¼ 小匙
　　薑酒汁……………… 1 小匙
　　太白粉……………… 1 大匙
　　蘆筍（去老皮）…… 30 公克
　②{ 熟筍…… 30 公克（約 1 兩）
　　香菇（泡軟）………… 2 朵
　　干瓢（12 公分長）… 12 條
　　高湯………………… 1 杯
　③{ 鹽………………… ⅓ 小匙
　　麻油……………… 1 小匙
　④{ 太白粉………… 1 ½ 小匙
　　水 ………………… 2 大匙

1/2 lb. (225 g.) fish meat
① { 1/4 t. salt
　 1 t. ginger wine
　 1 T. cornstarch
② { 1 oz. (30 g.) asparagus
　　 (peeled)
　 1 oz. (30 g.) bamboo
　　 shoots (cooked)
　 2 Chinese black
　　 mushrooms (soaked
　　 until soft)
　 12 dried gourd
　　 shavings (5" long)
③ { 1 c. broth
　 1/3 t. salt
　 1 t. sesame oil
④ { 1-1/2 t. cornstarch } mix
　 2 T. water

❶魚肉切薄片（5×4×0.5 公分），約 12 片，以①料醃 10 分鐘，蘆筍、熟筍、香菇均切 4 公分長條（各 12 條），干瓢泡軟備用。

❷取一片魚肉，擺上一份②料捲起，以干瓢綁緊，依次做好，水開以大火蒸熟（約 5 分鐘）取出排盤上。

❸③料煮滾，以④料勾芡，淋於魚捲上即成。

■可以紅蘿蔔、巴西利、生菜彩盤。

❶ Cut fish into about 12 thin slices, 2" x 1-1/2" x 1/4". Marinate in ① for 10 minutes. Slice asparagus, cooked bamboo shoots, and mushrooms into 1-1/2" long sticks (about 12 sticks each). Soak dried gourd shavings until soft and set aside.

❷ Place one stick each of ② on 1 slice of fish, roll up fish slices. Tie each roll tightly with 1 dried gourd shaving. Repeat this process until all are rolled and tied. Bring water to a boil. Steam fish rolls over high heat for about 5 minutes or until done. Remove from heat and arrange on plate.

❸ Bring ③ to a boil. Thicken with ④. Pour over fish rolls and serve immediately.

■ Carrots, parsley, and lettuce may be used as garnish.

鳳梨魚塊　PINEAPPLE AND FISH PIECES

營養含量 Nutritional Content		
蛋白質 Protein	（公克）(g)	4
脂　肪 Fat	（公克）(g)	9
醣 Carbohydrates	（公克）(g)	11
膽固醇 Cholesterol	（毫克）(mg)	10
熱　量 Calories	（大卡）(Cal)	141

1 人份　Per Serving

魚肉……… 80 公克(約 2 兩)
① 醬油………………… ½ 大匙
　薑酒汁…………… 1 小匙
　蛋黃…………………… ½ 個
太白粉…………… 2 小匙
鳳梨……… 150 公克(4 兩)
青椒… 50 公克(約 1 ½ 兩)
蒜末…………………… 1 小匙
② 糖……………………… 1 大匙
　醋……………………… 1 大匙
　番茄醬……………… 2 大匙
　水……………………… 3 大匙
　太白粉…………… ½ 小匙
沙拉油………………… 3 杯

2-3/4 oz. (80 g.) fish meat
1/2 T. soy sauce
① 1 t. ginger wine
1/2 egg yolk
2 t. cornstarch
1/3 lb. (150 g.) pineapple
1-3/4 oz. (50 g.) green pepper
1 t. garlic (minced)
1 T. sugar
1 T. vinegar
② 2 T. ketchup
3 T. water
1/2 t. cornstarch
3 c. vegetable oil

❶魚肉切塊(3×3×1 公分)，以①料醃 10 分鐘，炸前拌入太白粉，鳳梨切片青椒切塊備用。

❷油燒熱，入魚塊炸至金黃色(約 2 分鐘)取出，留油 1 大匙，將蒜末爆香，入鳳梨、青椒炒數下，隨入②料煮開，並下魚塊拌勻即刻盛出。

❶ Cut fish meat into 1-1/4″ x 1-1/4″ x 1/2″ pieces. Marinate in ① for 10 minutes. Dip each piece in cornstarch before frying. Slice pineapple. Cut green pepper into pieces. Set aside.

❷ Heat 3 c. oil in preheated wok. Add fish and deep-fry until golden (approx. 2 minutes). Remove fish, leaving 1 T. oil in wok. Stir-fry minced garlic until fragrant. Add pineapple and green pepper. Quickly stir-fry. Add ② and bring to a boil. Add fish pieces; stir until mixed well. Remove immediately and serve.

芹菜拌蟹腿 CELERY AND CRAB STRIPS

營養含量 Nutritional Content		
蛋白質 Protein	（公克）(g)	5
脂 肪 Fat	（公克）(g)	8
醣 Carbohydrates	（公克）(g)	4
膽固醇 Cholesterol	（毫克）(mg)	12
熱 量 Calories	（大卡）(Cal)	108

1 人份　Per Serving

西洋芹菜········· 200 公克
　　　　　　（約 5 ½ 兩）
鹽····················· ½ 小匙
仿蟹腿···· 90公克(約2 ½兩)
① 蒜泥················· 2 小匙
　　味精················· ⅛ 小匙
　　麻油················· 1 小匙
　　沙拉油··············· 1 大匙

1/2 lb. (200 g.) celery
1/2 t. salt
3 oz. (90 g.) imitation
　　crab legs
① 2 t. garlic paste
　 1 t. sesame oil
　 1 T. vegetable oil

❶芹菜切 5 公分長段，以滾水燙 1 分鐘取出，加鹽拌醃 20 分鐘，仿蟹腿剝成絲狀。

❷將所有材料拌上①料即可。

■芹菜應先去老筋。

❶ Chop celery into pieces, 2″ long. Boil for 1 minute; remove. Add salt and pickle for 20 minutes. Tear imitation crab legs into strips.

❷ Mix celery and crab strips with ① and serve.

■ Celery skin must be peeled before use.

瓜苗魚條　MELON SPROUTS AND FISH PIECES

營養含量 Nutritional Content		
蛋白質 Protein	（公克） (g)	4
脂　肪 Fat	（公克） (g)	10
醣 Carbohydrates	（公克） (g)	2
膽固醇 Cholesterol	（毫克） (mg)	10
熱　量 Calories	（大卡） (Cal)	114

1 人份　Per Serving

魚肉‥‥‥‥ 75 公克（2 兩）
① 酒‥‥‥‥‥‥‥‥‥‥ ½ 小匙
　 鹽‥‥‥‥‥‥‥‥‥‥ ⅛ 小匙
　 太白粉‥‥‥‥‥‥‥‥ ½ 大匙
隼人瓜苗‥‥‥‥‥ 200 公克
（或西洋芹菜，約 5 ½ 兩）
薑絲‥‥‥‥‥‥‥‥‥ 1 大匙
② 鹽‥‥‥‥‥‥‥‥‥‥ ½ 小匙
　 味精‥‥‥‥‥‥‥‥‥ ¼ 小匙
　 酒‥‥‥‥‥‥‥‥‥‥ 1 小匙
沙拉油‥‥‥‥‥‥‥‥ 2 大匙

2-2/3 oz. (75 g.) fish
　meat (red snapper,
　bluefish, or mackerel)
① 1/2 t. cooking wine
　 1/8 t. salt
　 1/2 T. cornstarch
　 1/2 lb. (200 g.) melon
　 sprouts (or celery)
　 1 T. shredded ginger
　 root
② 1/2 t. salt
　 1 t. cooking wine
　 2 T. vegetable oil

❶魚肉切條狀，加①料拌勻醃 10 分鐘，瓜苗切 5 公分長段備用。

❷油燒熱，將魚肉中火炒至變白取出，餘油炒香薑絲，續入瓜苗炒數下，加水 2
大匙稍燜軟（約 1 分鐘）再入魚條及②料炒勻即可。

■隼人瓜苗爲佛手瓜的嫩芽可以芹菜代替。

■爲增美觀，可撒少許紅辣椒絲點綴。

❶ Cut fish meat into rectangular pieces. Add ① and marinate for 10
minutes. Cut melon sprouts into 2″ long sections and set aside.

❷ Heat 2T. oil in preheated wok. Stir-fry fish over medium heat until white.
Remove from heat. In remaining oil, stir-fry ginger strips until fragrant. Add
melon sprouts and quickly stir-fry. Add 2 T. water; cover and cook over low
heat for about 1 minute. Add fish pieces and ②; stir to mix. Remove from
heat and serve.

■ Celery may be substituted for melon sprouts.

■ Shredded red chili pepper may be used as garnish.

瓜茄溜魚片
FISH SLICES WITH TOMATO AND CUCUMBER

營養含量 Nutritional Content		
蛋白質 Protein	（公克） (g)	4
脂　肪 Fat	（公克） (g)	10
醣 Carbohydrates	（公克） (g)	6
膽固醇 Cholesterol	（毫克） (mg)	10
熱　量 Calories	（大卡） (Cal)	130

1 人份　Per Serving

魚肉‥‥‥‥ 75 公克（ 2 兩）
① 鹽‥‥‥‥‥‥‥‥ ⅛ 小匙
　 薑酒汁‥‥‥‥‥‥ ½ 小匙
　 太白粉‥‥‥‥‥‥ 1 小匙
　 番茄(約 ½ 個)‥‥ 150 公克
　　　　　　　　 （ 4 兩）
　 小黃瓜‥ 80 公克(約 2 兩)
② 蔥（ 3 公分長）‥‥‥ 3 段
　 薑片‥‥‥‥‥‥‥‥ 3 片
　 鹽‥‥‥‥‥‥‥‥ ½ 小匙
　 糖‥‥‥‥‥‥‥‥ 1 大匙
③ 醋‥‥‥‥‥‥‥‥ 2 大匙
　 麻油‥‥‥‥‥‥‥ ½ 小匙
　 太白粉‥‥‥‥‥‥ 1 小匙
　 水‥‥‥‥‥‥‥‥ ½ 杯
　 沙拉油‥‥‥‥‥‥ 2 大匙

2-2/3 oz. (75 g.) fish meat
① 1/8 t. salt
　 1/2 t. ginger wine
　 1 t. cornstarch
　 1/3 lb. (150 g.) tomato
　　 (about 1/2)
　 2-2/3 oz. (80 g.) gherkin
　　 cucumber
　　 (about 75 g.)
② 3 sections green onion
　　 (1-1/4")
　 3 slices ginger root
　 1/2 t. salt
　 1 T. sugar
　 2 T. vinegar
③ 1/2 t. sesame oil
　 1 t. cornstarch
　 1/2 c. water
　 2 T. vegetable oil

❶魚肉切（ 4×3×0.5 公分）片狀，加①料醃 10 分鐘，番茄、小黃瓜切片狀備用。
❷油燒熱，入魚片炒至變色即刻取出，餘油將②料爆香，下番茄、小黃瓜炒數下，隨入③料煮滾，並入魚片拌勻即可。

❶ Cut fish meat into 1-1/2" x 1-1/4" x 1/4" pieces. Add ① and marinate for 10 minutes. Slice tomatoes and gherkin cucumbers. Set aside.
❷ Heat 2 T. oil in preheated wok. Add fish and stir-fry until color changes. Remove immediately. In remaining oil, stir-fry ② until fragrant. Add tomatoes and cucumbers. Quickly stir-fry. Add ③ and bring to a boil. Add fish; stir to mix. Remove from heat and serve.

翡翠蝦球　EMERALD SHRIMP BALLS

營養含量 Nutritional Content		
蛋白質 Protein	（公克） (g)	4
脂　肪 Fat	（公克） (g)	11
醣 Carbohydrates	（公克） (g)	2
膽固醇 Cholesterol	（毫克） (mg)	28
熱　量 Calories	（大卡） (Cal)	123

1 人份　Per Serving

蝦仁……… 75 公克 (2 兩)
① ⎰ 鹽……………………… ⅙ 小匙
　　薑酒汁………………… ¼ 小匙
　　蛋白…………………… ⅓ 個
　⎱ 太白粉………………… ½ 小匙
青花菜………… 200 公克
　　　　　　（約 5 ½ 兩）
蒜末………………… 1 小匙
② ⎰ 鹽………………… ⅓ 小匙
　　味精……………… ¼ 小匙
　⎱ 水………………… 1 大匙
沙拉油………………… ½ 杯

2-2/3 oz. (75 g.) shrimp
　(shelled)
① { 1/6 t. salt
　　1/4 t. ginger wine
　　1/3 egg white
　　1/2 t. cornstarch
1/2 lb. (200 g.) broccoli
1 t. garlic (minced)
② { 1/3 t. salt
　　1 T. water
1/2 c. vegetable oil

❶蝦仁去腸泥洗淨，由背部切開（不要切斷），加①料拌勻醃 10 分鐘，青花菜切小朵，以滾水川燙 30 秒取出。

❷油 ½ 杯燒熱，將蝦仁以中火過油至變色取出（約九分熟），留油 2 大匙，蒜末爆香，入青花菜、蝦仁及②料速炒均勻即可。

❶ Devein shrimp; rinse. Cut along backside of shrimp; do not cut through. Marinate shrimp in ① for 10 minutes. Cut broccoli into small pieces and blanch in boiling water for 30 seconds. Remove from heat.

❷ Heat 1/2 c. oil over high heat in preheated wok. Reduce heat to medium and add shrimp; stir-fry until color changes Remove shrimp, leaving 2 T. oil in wok. Add garlic and stir-fry until fragrant. Add broccoli, shrimp and ② . Stir-fry quickly until done. Serve.

金針虱目魚湯
TIGER LILY AND MILKFISH SOUP

營養含量 Nutritional Content		
蛋白質 Protein	（公克） (g)	4
脂　肪 Fat	（公克） (g)	3
醣 Carbohydrates	（公克） (g)	1
膽固醇 Cholesterol	（毫克） (mg)	10
熱　量 Calories	（大卡） (Cal)	47

1 人份　Per Serving

	虱目魚·············	100 公克
		（約 2 ½ 兩）
	金針·····	10 公克（約 ¼ 兩）
①	水·························	5 杯
	酒······················	1 小匙
	鹽·····················	⅔ 小匙
	薑絲·················	1 大匙
	蔥花·················	1 大匙

1/4 lb. (100 g.) milkfish
1/3 oz. (10 g.) dried tiger lily
① 5 c. water
1 t. cooking wine
2/3 t. salt
1 T. shredded ginger root
1 T. green onion (chopped)

❶虱目魚斜切成塊，金針泡軟備用。

❷虱目魚、金針置燉盅中，加①料入蒸鍋，水開以大火蒸約 30 分鐘取出，撒上蔥花即可。

■可以電鍋（外鍋加水 1 杯）蒸熟。

❶ Diagonally cut milkfish into pieces. Soak dried tiger lily in water until soft and set aside.

❷ Place milkfish and tiger lily in stewing pot. Add ①. Place in steaming pot and steam over boiling water for about 30 minutes . Remove from heat. Sprinkle with chopped green onion and serve.

■ If electric rice cooker is used, place one cup of water in outer pot.

西洋菜魚片湯
WATERCRESS AND FISH SOUP

營養含量 Nutritional Content		
蛋白質 Protein	（公克） (g)	4
脂　肪 Fat	（公克） (g)	3
醣 Carbohydrates	（公克） (g)	2
膽固醇 Cholesterol	（毫克） (mg)	10
熱　量 Calories	（大卡） (Cal)	51

1 人份　Per Serving

魚肉········ 75 公克(2 兩)
① 鹽······················ ¼ 小匙
　酒······················ ½ 小匙
　太白粉················· 1 小匙
西洋菜····· 150 公克(4 兩)
② 水······················· 5 杯
　嫩薑絲··············· 1 大匙
③ 酒······················ ½ 小匙
　鹽······················ 1 小匙
　麻油·················· ½ 小匙

2-2/3 oz. (75 g.) fish meat
　1/4 t. salt
① 1/2 t. cooking wine
　1 t. cornstarch
　1/3 lb. (150 g.)
　　watercress
② 5 c. water
　1 T. shredded baby
　　ginger root
　1/2 t. cooking wine
③ 1 t. salt
　1/2 t. sesame oil

❶魚肉切片（ 4×3×0.5 公分），加①料醃 10 分鐘，西洋菜切 5 公分長段。

❷將②料煮開，下西洋菜、魚片大火煮滾，以③料調味即可。

❶ Cut fish meat into thin slices, 1-1/2'' x 1-1/4'' x 1/4'' pieces. Add ① and marinate for 10 minutes. Cut watercress into 2'' long sections.

❷ Bring ② to a boil. Add watercress and fish meat. Bring to a boil over high heat. Season with ③ and serve.

■ Ginger root may be substituted for baby ginger root.

黃豆及油類

1. 好處多多的黃豆

黃豆是植物蛋白質中的佼佼者。其脂質所含之不飽和脂肪酸、主要脂肪酸及卵磷脂的量均比動物性脂肪爲高，足以幫助降低血中膽固醇；而且黃豆內含一種植物固醇，爲肉類食物所無，能與膽固醇相競爭消化，進而抑制其吸收；再者，其所含之纖維質，不僅可降低血中膽固醇，同時可改善便秘。

雖然黃豆堅硬無味，烹調菜式又少，遠不如其製品（如豆漿、豆腐等）受歡迎，但是它在降低血中膽固醇、預防便秘、大腸癌及心血管疾病的功能上卻超越甚多，若能善加利用則受益匪淺！

2. 烹調時別忘了植物油。

植物油中，除了椰子油及棕櫚油外，我們經常使用的植物油（如大豆油、玉米油、葵花籽油和花生油等），不僅不飽和脂肪含量高出動物油很多，甚至所含的主要脂肪酸亦爲食物之冠。

主要脂肪酸的功能除降低血中膽固醇外，尚有調節血壓、防止血液凝結、傳遞神經衝動、刺激平滑肌的收縮、維持細胞膜及血管結構完整等。而最受重視的是促進生長發育及保護皮膚的完整，以免受濕疹之苦。又植物油含維生素 E 較多，可防止不飽和脂肪酸的氧化，也具有預防細胞膜及皮膚老化的效能。若烹調時不用植物油，則體內不飽和脂肪酸有不足之虞，而無法執行其生理作用，且使體內飽和脂肪酸過多，導致血脂肪及血膽固醇高，易罹患或加重心血管性疾病。所以烹調時別忘了用植物油，以彌補葷菜、點心所含不飽和脂肪酸之不足，即可擁有健康的身體及美麗的皮膚。

SOYBEANS AND OILS

1. SOYBEANS—MANY NUTRITIONAL BENEFITS

Soybeans provide the best source of plant proteins. The amount of unsaturated fatty acids, essential fatty acids, and lecithin contained in soybeans is higher than that contained in animal fats. Soybeans are capable of reducing cholesterol in the blood; Furthermore, soybeans contain a type of phytosterol which is lacking in meats. This phytosterol competes with cholesterol in the digestive process, thereby restraining its absorption. The fiber contained in soybeans cannot only reduce the cholesterol in the blood but can also reduce constipation.

Although soybeans are hard, tasteless, and rarely used in Chinese cooking, not to mention their not being nearly as popular as their products (such as soybean milk, bean curd, etc), they prove highly effective in reducing blood cholesterol as well as in preventing constipation, cancer of the large intestine, and cardiovascular diseases. If readers are able to add soybeans to their diet, they will receive countless benefits.

2. WHEN PREPARING FOOD, DON'T FORGET VEGETABLE OILS

Among vegetable oils, besides coconut oil and palm oil, those which we use regularly (such as soybean oil, corn oil, sunflower, and peanut oil, etc.) contain many more unsaturated fatty acids than do animal oils. Among all foods, vegetable oils are the best providers of essential fatty acids.

Besides their function of reducing blood cholesterol, essential fatty acids can also moderate blood pressure, prevent blood coagulation, and transmit nerve impulses. Essential fatty acids also stimulate the smooth contraction of muscles, thereby maintaining the complete structure of the cell walls. That function which is most highly stressed is essential fatty acids' ability to promote growth and protect the integrity of the skin, the latter function of which guards against Eczema. As vegetable oils contain a larger amount of vitamin E, they can hinder the oxidation of unsaturated fatty acids and also prevent the aging of the cellular walls and the skin.

If vegetable oils are not used in preparing foods, it is possible that the body won't absorb a sufficient amount of unsaturated fatty acids. This ,in turn, will not allow the body to effectively execute its own physiological functions. The body will also contain an excess of saturated fatty acids which leads to high levels of fat and cholesterol in the blood. This increases one's chances of contracting cardiovascular diseases. Therefore, when preparing foods, don't forget to include vegetable oils to supplement the insufficient amount of unsaturated fatty acids contained in meat dishes and desserts. With vegetable oils as part of your diet, you will enjoy a healthy body and beautiful skin.

黃豆燉牛肉 SOY BEAN AND BEEF STEW

營養含量 Nutritional Content		
蛋白質 Protein	（公克） (g)	12
脂　肪 Fat	（公克） (g)	12
醣 Carbohydrates	（公克） (g)	1
膽固醇 Cholesterol	（毫克） (mg)	34
熱　量 Calories	（大卡） (Cal)	160

1 人份　Per Serving

黃豆… 50 公克(約 1 ½ 兩)
牛腱肉⋯⋯ 150 公克(4 兩)
番茄⋯100 公克(約 2 ½ 兩)
① 蒜頭(拍碎)⋯⋯⋯⋯⋯ 3 粒
　　薑⋯⋯⋯⋯⋯⋯⋯⋯ 2 片
　　水⋯⋯⋯⋯⋯⋯⋯⋯ 6 杯
② 酒⋯⋯⋯⋯⋯⋯⋯ 1 大匙
　　醬油⋯⋯⋯⋯⋯⋯ 2 大匙
③ 太白粉⋯⋯⋯⋯⋯ 2 小匙
　　水⋯⋯⋯⋯⋯⋯⋯ 1 大匙
沙拉油⋯⋯⋯⋯⋯⋯ 1 大匙

1-3/4 oz. (50 g.)
　　soybeans
1/3 lb. (150 g.) beef
　　shank
1/4 lb. (100 g.) tomatoes
①{ 3 cloves garlic
　　　(crushed)
　　2 slices ginger root
　　6 c. water
②{ 1 T. cooking wine
　　2 T. soy sauce
③{ 2 t. cornstarch } mix
　　1 T. water
1 T. vegetable oil

❶黃豆以水泡軟(約 4 小時)，牛肉、番茄切塊備用。

❷油 1 大匙燒熱，將①料爆香，加水煮開，入牛肉、黃豆及②料煮滾後改小火燜煮 1 小時，入番茄再煮 10 分鐘以③料勾芡即可。

❶ Soak soybeans in water until soft (about 4 hours). Cut beef and tomatoes into pieces and set aside.

❷ Heat 1 T. oil in preheated wok. Quickly stir-fry ① until fragrant. Add water and bring to a boil. Add beef, soybeans, and ②. Bring to a boil, reduce heat, and simmer for 1 hour. Add tomatoes and simmer for 10 more minutes. Thicken with ③ and serve.

青蒜燒豆腐 COOKED CHIVES AND BEAN CURD

營養含量 Nutritional Content		
蛋白質 Protein	（公克） (g)	8
脂　肪 Fat	（公克） (g)	13
醣 Carbohydrates	（公克） (g)	2
膽固醇 Cholesterol	（毫克） (mg)	8
熱　量 Calories	（大卡） (Cal)	157

1 人份　Per Serving

豆腐 3 塊‥300 公克(8 兩)
蒜苗‥‥‥‥‥‥‥ 2 枝
絞肉‥ 50 公克(約 1 ½ 兩)
① { 高湯‥‥‥‥‥‥‥ ¾ 杯
醬油‥‥‥‥‥‥‥ ¼ 小匙
糖‥‥‥‥‥‥‥‥ ½ 小匙
麻油‥‥‥‥‥‥‥ ½ 小匙
② { 太白粉‥‥‥‥‥‥ 1 小匙
水‥‥‥‥‥‥‥‥ 1 大匙
沙拉油‥‥‥‥‥‥ 2 大匙

2/3 lb. (300 g.) bean
　curd (3 squares)
2 stalks leek
1-3/4 oz. (50 g.) ground
　pork
① { 3/4 c. broth
1/4 t. soy sauce
1/2 t. sugar
1/2 t. sesame oil
② { 1 t. cornstarch
1 T. water } mix
2 T. vegetable oil

❶豆腐切約 2 公分方塊，蒜苗切斜段。

❷油 2 大匙燒熱，將絞肉炒鬆，入蒜白炒香，隨入豆腐及①料，煮滾後改小火燜煮 5 分鐘，再放入蒜青，並以②料勾芡即可。

■如無青蒜可改用大蔥。

❶ Cut bean curd into pieces, 3/4" square. Slice leek diagonally.

❷ Heat 2T.oil in preheated wok.Stir-fry ground pork until it separates.Add white part of chives and stir-fry until fragrant. Add bean curd and①. Bring to a boil, reduce heat, and simmer for 5 minutes.Add green part of chives, thicken with ② and serve.

■ Green onion may be substituted for leek.

香菇豆腐　MUSHROOMS AND BEAN CURD

營養含量 Nutritional Content		
蛋白質 Protein	（公克）(g)	8
脂　肪 Fat	（公克）(g)	14
醣 Carbohydrates	（公克）(g)	1
膽固醇 Cholesterol	（毫克）(mg)	6
熱　量 Calories	（大卡）(Cal)	162

1 人份　Per Serving

豆腐……4 塊（約 400 公克）

① 香菇…………………… 3 朵
　蝦米…………………… 1 大匙
　葱（ 3 公分長）……… 3 段

② 高湯…………………… 2 杯
　醬油…………………… 2 大匙
　糖……………………… 1 小匙
　胡椒…………………… ⅛ 小匙
　麻油…………………… ½ 小匙

③ 太白粉………………… 1 大匙
　水……………………… 3 大匙

沙拉油………………… 3 杯

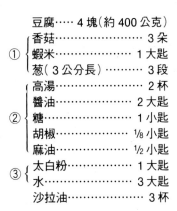

4 squares 14-1/4 oz. (or 400 g.) bean curd

① 3 Chinese black mushrooms
1 T. dried shrimp
3 sections green onion (1-1/4")

② 2 c. broth
2 T. soy sauce
1 t. sugar
1/8 t. pepper
1/2 t. sesame oil

③ 1 T. cornstarch
3 T. water　} mix

3 c. vegetable oil

❶豆腐每塊橫切成 2 大片，香菇泡軟切片，蝦米泡水 5 分鐘取出。

❷油燒至十分熱，入豆腐炸成金黃色取出，留油 1 大匙，將①料爆香，再入②料及豆腐煮開，改小火燜煮 5 分鐘，以③料勾芡即可。

■可以香菜點綴。

❶ Cut each square of bean curd lengthwise into two pieces, about 1/3" thick. Soak mushrooms in water until soft and slice. Soak dried shrimp in water for 5 minutes; remove and drain.

❷ Heat 3 c. oil in preheated wok. Add bean curd and deep-fry until golden. Remove from heat. Leave 1 T. oil in wok. Stir-fry ① until fragrant. Add ② and bean curd. Bring to a boil. Reduce heat and simmer for 5 minutes. Thicken with ③ and serve.

■Coriander may be used as garnish.

香干牛肉　PRESSED BEAN CURD AND BEEF

營養含量 Nutritional Content		
蛋白質 Protein	（公克） (g)	9
脂　肪 Fat	（公克） (g)	14
醣 Carbohydrates	（公克） (g)	1
膽固醇 Cholesterol	（毫克） (mg)	27
熱　量 Calories	（大卡） (Cal)	166

1 人份　Per Serving

牛肉……120 公克（約 3 兩）
① 薑酒汁……………… 1 小匙
　 醬油………………… 1 小匙
　 太白粉……………… 2 小匙
② 五香豆干……… 90 公克
　　　　　　　（約 2½ 兩）
　 青椒……… 75 公克（2 兩）
　 紅辣椒…10 公克（約¼ 兩）
③ 葱（3 公分長）……… 3 段
　 薑絲……………… 1 大匙
④ 鹽………………… ⅓ 小匙
　 糖………………… ¼ 小匙
　 麻油……………… ½ 小匙
　 酒………………… ½ 小匙
　 太白粉…………… 1 小匙
　 水………………… 3 大匙
　 沙拉油…………… 2 大匙

1/4 lb. (120 g.) beef
① 1 t. ginger wine
　 1 t. soy sauce
　 2 t. cornstarch
② 3-1/4 oz. (90 g.) pressed
　　 bean curd
　 2-2/3 oz. (75 g.) green
　　 pepper
　 1/3 oz. (10 g.) red chili
　　 pepper
③ 3 sections green onion
　　 (1-1/4″)
　 1 T. shredded ginger
　　 root
④ 1/3 t. salt
　 1/4 t. sugar
　 1/2 t. sesame oil
　 1/2 t. cooking wine
　 1 t. cornstarch
　 3 T. water
　 2 T. vegetable oil

❶牛肉橫紋切絲，加①料拌勻，②料亦切絲備用。

❷油燒熱，入牛肉炒至變色取出，餘油炒香③料，下②料炒數下，隨入牛肉及④料炒勻即可。

❶ Slice beef against the grain into strips. Add ① and mix well. Cut ② into strips and set aside.

❷ Heat 2 T. oil in preheated wok. Add beef and stir-fry until color changes. Remove from heat. In remaining oil, stir-fry ③ until fragrant. Add ② and rapidly stir-fry. Add beef and ④; stir-fry until mixed well. Remove from heat and serve.

豆腐丸子　BEAN CURD BALLS

4 人份　Serves 4

營養含量 Nutritional Content		
蛋白質 Protein	（公克） (g)	8
脂　肪 Fat	（公克） (g)	12
醣 Carbohydrates	（公克） (g)	5
膽固醇 Cholesterol	（毫克） (mg)	18
熱　量 Calories	（大卡） (Cal)	160

1 人份　Per Serving

豆腐……… 150 公克(4 兩)
豬絞肉………… 100 公克
　　　　　（約 2 ½ 兩）
① 　鹽……………… ½ 小匙
糖……………… ½ 小匙
蛋白……………… ½ 個
葱、薑末……… 各 1 小匙
太白粉…………… 1 大匙
麻油…………… ½ 小匙
麵包粉…………… ½ 杯
沙拉油…………… 3 杯

1/3 lb. (150 g.) bean
　curd
1/4 lb. (100 g.) ground
　pork
① 　1/2 t. salt
1/2 t. sugar
1/2 egg white
1 t. green onion
　(minced)
1 t. ginger root
　(minced)
1 T. cornstarch
1/2 t. sesame oil
1/2 c. bread crumbs
3 c. vegetable oil

❶豆腐吸乾水份以刀壓成泥狀，加絞肉及①料拌勻，做成丸子狀（約 20 個），沾上麵包粉備用。

❷油燒至八分熱，入丸子以中火炸熟並呈金黃色（約 3 分鐘）取出，趁熱食用即可。

■可以番茄、生菜葉彩盤。

■豆腐宜買水份較少的老豆腐。

❶ Dry bean curd with paper towel and mash with knife. Add ground pork and ①. Mix evenly and form about 20 balls. Roll each ball into bread crumbs and set aside.

❷ Heat 3 c. oil in preheated wok. Add balls and deep-fry over medium heat until golden brown (about 3 minutes). Remove with slotted spoon and serve while hot.

■ Tomato and lettuce may be used as garnish.

■ Dryer bean curd is more suitable for this recipe.

百葉結燒肉 BEAN CURD KNOTS AND PORK

營養含量 Nutritional Content		
蛋白質 Protein	（公克） (g)	10
脂　肪 Fat	（公克） (g)	13
醣 Carbohydrates	（公克） (g)	3
膽固醇 Cholesterol	（毫克） (mg)	20
熱　量 Calories	（大卡） (Cal)	169

1 人份　Per Serving

①
豬腿肉‥120 公克（約 3 兩）
百葉結 60 公克（約 1 ½ 兩）
海帶結 90 公克（約 2 ½ 兩）
紅蘿蔔 50 公克（約 1 ½ 兩）

②
薑‥‥‥‥‥‥‥‥‥ 3 片
葱（ 3 公分長）‥‥‥‥ 4 段
蒜頭（拍碎）‥‥‥‥‥ 3 粒

③
水‥‥‥‥‥‥‥‥‥ 3 杯
醬油‥‥‥‥‥‥‥‥ 3 大匙
糖‥‥‥‥‥‥‥‥‥ 1 小匙
酒‥‥‥‥‥‥‥‥‥ 1 大匙
沙拉油‥‥‥‥‥‥ 1 ½ 大匙

1/4 lb. (120 g.) boneless
　pork leg roast
①
2 oz. (60 g.) bean curd
　wrapper knots
3-1/4 oz. (90 g.) seaweed
　knots
1-3/4 oz. (50 g.) carrots

②
3 slices ginger root
4 sections green onion,
　1-1/4"
3 cloves garlic (crushed)

③
3 c. water
3 T. soy sauce
1 t. sugar
1 T. cooking wine
1-1/2 T. vegetable oil

❶腿肉切塊（ 5 公分×3 公分×3 公分），紅蘿蔔切滾刀塊備用。

❷油燒熱，下②料爆香，入腿肉略炒，再加①料同炒，隨入③料大火煮開，改小火燜煮 40 分鐘即可。

❶ Cut pork leg into pieces, 2" x 1-1/4" x 1-1/4". Dice carrots and set aside.

❷ Heat 1-1/2T. oil in preheated wok. Quickly stir-fry ② until fragrant. Add pork; stir. Add ① and quickly stir-fry. Add ③ and bring to a boil. Reduce heat and simmer for 40 minutes. Serve.

韭黃豆包　CHIVES AND BEAN CURD STRIPS

營養含量 Nutritional Content		
蛋白質 Protein	（公克） (g)	6
脂　肪 Fat	（公克） (g)	12
醣 Carbohydrates	（公克） (g)	2
膽固醇 Cholesterol	（毫克） (mg)	0
熱　量 Calories	（大卡） (Cal)	140

1 人份　Per Serving

韭黃‥200 公克（約 5 ½ 兩）
炸豆包‥‥‥‥ 75 公克（ 2 兩）
蔥絲‥‥‥‥‥‥‥‥‥ 1 大匙
紅蘿蔔絲 20 公克（約 ½ 兩）
① { 鹽‥‥‥‥‥‥‥‥‥ ⅓ 小匙
　 味精‥‥‥‥‥‥‥‥ ¼ 小匙
沙拉油‥‥‥‥‥‥‥ 2 大匙

1/2 lb. (200 g.) yellow
　Chinese chives
2-2/3 oz. (75 g.) fried
　bean curd pockets
1 T. shredded green
　onion
3/4 oz. (20 g.) carrot
　(strips)
1/3 t. salt
2 T. vegetable oil

❶韭黃切段，豆包切絲。

❷油 2 大匙燒熱，入蔥絲、韭黃炒香，再下豆包、紅蘿蔔絲炒片刻，以①料調味即可。

■豆包可改用空心油炸豆腐或豆干代替。

❶ Cut chives into sections. Cut bean curd pockets into strips.

❷ Heat 2 T. oil in preheated wok. Add green onion and chives. Stir-fry until fragrant. Add bean curd pocket strips and carrot strips; stir to mix. Season with 1/3 t. salt and serve.

■ Pressed bean curd or deep fried bean curd may be substituted for bean curd pockets.

百葉筍湯
BEAN CURD WRAPPER AND BAMBOO SHOOT SOUP

營養含量 Nutritional Content		
蛋白質 Protein	（公克） (g)	6
脂 肪 Fat	（公克） (g)	4
醣 Carbohydrates	（公克） (g)	2
膽固醇 Cholesterol	（毫克） (mg)	5
熱 量 Calories	（大卡） (Cal)	68

1 人份　Per Serving

筍⋯⋯ 200 公克(約 5½ 兩)
百葉結 50 公克(約 1½ 兩)
香菇⋯⋯⋯⋯⋯⋯⋯ 3 朵
中式火腿 20 公克(約 ½ 兩)
① 高湯⋯⋯⋯⋯⋯⋯⋯ 7 杯
　 鹽⋯⋯⋯⋯⋯⋯⋯ 1 小匙
　 味精⋯⋯⋯⋯⋯⋯ ¼ 小匙

1/2 lb. (200 g.) bamboo shoots
1-3/4 oz. (50 g.) bean curd wrapper knots
3 Chinese black mushrooms
3/4 oz. (20 g.) Chinese-style ham
① { 7 c. broth
　 1 t. salt

❶筍切滾刀塊，香菇泡軟切片，火腿蒸熟切薄片。
❷①料煮開，下筍塊、百葉結、香菇及火腿，待滾，改小火燜煮 30 分鐘即可。
■如無百葉結可用油豆腐取代。

❶ Dice bamboo shoots. Soak mushrooms in water until soft and slice. Steam ham for 10 minutes and thinly slice.

❷ Bring ① to a boil. Add bamboo shoot pieces, bean curd wrapper, Chinese black mushrooms and ham. Bring to another boil, reduce heat and simmer for 30 minutes. Serve.

■ Deep-fried bean curd may be substituted for bean curd wrapper knots.

榨菜豆腐湯
MUSTARD GREEN AND BEAN CURD SOUP

4 人份　Serves 4

營養含量 Nutritional Content		
蛋白質　（公克） Protein　（g）	4
脂　肪　（公克） Fat　（g）	3
醣　　　（公克） Carbohydrates　（g）	2
膽固醇　（毫克） Cholesterol　（mg）	0
熱　量　（大卡） Calories　（Cal）	47

1 人份　Per Serving

榨菜‥100 公克（約 2 ½ 兩）
豆腐 2 塊‥‥‥‥‥ 200 公克
　　　　　　　（約 5 ½ 兩）
高湯‥‥‥‥‥‥‥‥ 5 杯
① ⎰ 鹽‥‥‥‥‥‥‥‥ ¼ 小匙
　⎱ 醬油‥‥‥‥‥‥‥ 2 小匙
葱花‥‥‥‥‥‥‥‥ 1 大匙

1/4 lb. (100 g.) Szechuan
　pickled mustard green
1/2 lb. (200 g.) bean
　curd (2 squares)
5 c. broth
① ⎰ 1/4 t. salt
　⎱ 2 t. soy sauce
　1 T. green onion
　　(chopped)

❶榨菜切 2 公分正方薄片，豆腐切 2 公分丁塊。

❷榨菜放入高湯中煮開，下豆腐煮滾，並以①料調味，盛碗中，撒上葱花即可。

■榨菜較鹹時，可不必再加鹽。

❶ Cut mustard green into thin slices, 3/4″ thick. Cut bean curd into 3/4″ cubes.

❷ Place mustard green in broth and bring to a boil. Add bean curd and bring to another boil. Season with ①. Pour into serving bowl and sprinkle with chopped green onion.

■ If mustard green is too salty, salt may be omitted from recipe.

高麗豆腐湯 CABBAGE AND BEAN CURD SOUP

營養含量 Nutritional Content		
蛋白質 Protein	（公克） (g)	4
脂　肪 Fat	（公克） (g)	3
醣 Carbohydrates	（公克） (g)	1
膽固醇 Cholesterol	（毫克） (mg)	0
熱　量 Calories	（大卡） (Cal)	47

1 人份　Per Serving

豆腐⋯⋯⋯⋯⋯⋯⋯ 2 塊
高麗菜⋯⋯⋯⋯ 100 公克
　　　　（約 2 ½ 兩）
① ⎰ 高湯⋯⋯⋯⋯⋯⋯⋯ 5 杯
　 ⎨ 鹽⋯⋯⋯⋯⋯⋯⋯ 1 小匙
　 ⎱ 柴魚精⋯⋯⋯⋯⋯ ¼ 小匙

2 squares (7 oz. or
　200 g.) bean curd
1/4 lb. (100 g.) Chinese
　cabbage
① ⎰ 5 c. broth
　 ⎨ 1 t. salt
　 ⎩ 1/4 t. dried bonito
　　　essence (dashi)

❶豆腐切長方塊（ 3 公分× 2 公分× 5 公分），高麗菜切大片（約 5 公分正方）。
❷將①料煮開，入高麗菜及豆腐煮滾即可起鍋。
■高麗菜亦可以大白菜、小白菜、菠菜等代替。
■若無柴魚精可不加，或改用柴魚 2 大匙。

❶ Cut bean curd into rectangular pieces (1-1/4″ x 3/4″ x 2″). Cut cabbage into large slices (about 2″ square).

❷ Bring ① to a boil. Add cabbage and bean curd. Bring to another boil. Remove from heat and serve.

■Chinese Nappa cabbage, white Chinese cabbage, or spinach etc. may be substituted for cabbage.

■ Dried bonito essence may be omitted if unavailable or 2 T. dried bonito shavings may be used as substitute.

蛋與奶類 EGGS AND DAIRY PRODUCTS

1. 經濟實惠的蛋

一個蛋的營養價值與 30 公克煮熟的肉類相當，但其所含蛋白質的品質卻居所有動植物之冠。

蛋含有肉類所沒有的卵磷脂[註]，不僅可促進脂肪的消化作用，也可將血液中的膽固醇帶到其他器官組織，以降低血中膽固醇。雖然蛋所含的膽固醇稍高，但每日食用一個亦不足懼，因其只是人體本身膽固醇製造量的 1 / 6 ～ 1 / 5，這種經濟實惠的食物，應當每日食用。

2. 防止骨質疏鬆及軟化的主要來源～奶類

骨質疏鬆及軟化的病因固然有許多，但影響最大的是鈣質的缺乏。而奶類及其製品是蛋白質與鈣質的主要來源，單只一杯鮮奶即含有 280 毫克的鈣質，而均衡飲食中每日五大類食物（除奶類外）含鈣量的總和，僅供給 200 ～ 300 毫克。因此，若無飲用奶類，需加倍所有的食物，才能達到每日鈣質的建議量 600 毫克。

每日飲用一杯牛奶，使幼小者生長快速，年老者免受肌骨之疼；尤其更年期的婦女，因內分泌的變化，容易導致骨質疏鬆，更需要每日飲用，以確保健康。

註：卵磷脂是一種脂肪，屬於磷脂類，具有混合水和油的乳化作用。

1. EGGS—A BENEFICIAL PROTEIN SOURCE

The nutritional value of an egg is equivalent to that contained in 1 oz. (30 g.) of cooked meat. Yet the value of the protein it contains is the highest among all animals and plants.

Lecithin✳, which is contained in eggs but not in meats, can not only promote the function of fat digestion but also transport the cholesterol in the blood to other organs in order to reduce blood cholesterol. One need not worry about consuming one egg per day because it accounts for only 1/6-1/5 of the cholesterol volume manufactured in the human body. This type of nutritionally valuable food should be consumed daily.

2. DAIRY PRODUCTS—THE MOST IMPORTANT SOURCES OF NUTRITION WHICH GUARD AGAINST OSTEOPOROSIS AND OSTEOMALACIA

There are many causes of osteoporosis and osteomalacia, but that which serves as the greatest promoter of their development is calcium deficiency. Furthermore, milk and its products are essential sources of both protein and calcium. Just one cup of fresh milk contains 280 mg. of calcium. Furthermore, in a balanced diet one's daily intake of 5 food groups (besides milk products) supplies only 200-300 mg. of calcium. Therefore, if dairy products aren't a part of one's diet, one must consume double the amount of other foods in order to achieve the recommended daily calcium allowance of 600 mg.

Drinking one cup of milk every day enables children to grow quickly and helps the elderly to guard against osteoporosis; Elderly women especially require milk products in order to guarantee their health because changes in endocrine easily lead to osteoporosis.

✳ Lecithin: a type of fat in the phospholipid group which emulsifies water and oil.

蛋拌豆腐　EGG AND BEAN CURD SALAD

4 人份　Serves 4

營養含量 Nutritional Content		
蛋白質 Protein	（公克） (g)	11
脂　肪 Fat	（公克） (g)	9
醣 Carbohydrates	（公克） (g)	3
膽固醇 Cholesterol	（毫克） (mg)	125
熱　量 Calories	（大卡） (Cal)	137

1 人份　Per Serving

① 白煮蛋（或皮蛋）……… 2 個
豆腐 400 公克（約 10 ½ 兩）
番茄‥100 公克（約 2 ½ 兩）
蘿蔔嬰…20 公克（約 ½ 兩）

② 醬油（淡色）……… 1 ½ 大匙
麻油……………… ½ 大匙
糖………………… 1 小匙
醋………………… 1 小匙
蔥花……………… 1 大匙

① 2 hard-boiled eggs (or thousand-year-old eggs)
1 lb. (400 g.) bean curd
1/4 lb. (100 g.) tomatoes
3/4 oz. (20 g.) white radish sprouts

② 1-1/2 T. soy sauce
1/2 T. sesame oil
1 t. sugar
1 t. vinegar
1 T. green onion (chopped)

❶將蛋切圓片，豆腐及番茄切 2 公分丁塊備用。

❷①料全部置盤中，食時淋②料拌勻即可。

■電鍋煮蛋法：蛋直接放入電鍋中（不用內鍋），加水 2 大匙按下開關，至開關跳起即可，喜食全熟者，可續燜約 5 分鐘。

❶ Cut eggs into circular slices. Cut bean curd and tomatoes into 3/4" cubes and set aside.

❷ Place ① on serving plate. Pour on evenly mixed ② and serve.

■How to cook eggs in electric rice cooker: Place eggs directly into electric rice cooker (don't use inner pot). Add 2 T. water and flip switch down to turn on. When switch pops up, it's ready. For those who enjoy their eggs well-done, keep egg in cooker for 5 minutes after switch pops up.

醬瓜汁蒸蛋 STEAMED EGGS IN CUCUMBER JUICE

營養含量 Nutritional Content		
蛋白質 Protein	（公克） (g)	7
脂　肪 Fat	（公克） (g)	9
醣 Carbohydrates	（公克） (g)	—
膽固醇 Cholesterol	（毫克） (mg)	250
熱　量 Calories	（大卡） (Cal)	109

1 人份　Per Serving

蛋‧‧‧‧‧‧‧‧‧‧‧‧‧‧‧‧ 4 個

① 水‧‧‧‧‧‧‧‧‧‧‧‧‧‧‧ 2 ½ 杯
醬瓜汁‧‧‧‧‧‧‧‧‧‧ 3 大匙
（或醬油‧‧‧‧‧‧‧‧ 2 大匙）
鹽‧‧‧‧‧‧‧‧‧‧‧‧‧‧‧ ½ 小匙
蒜泥‧‧‧‧‧‧‧‧‧‧‧‧‧ 1 小匙
熟油‧‧‧‧‧‧‧‧‧‧‧‧‧ 1 大匙

② 高湯‧‧‧‧‧‧‧‧‧‧‧‧‧ 1 杯
鹽‧‧‧‧‧‧‧‧‧‧‧‧‧‧‧ ¼ 小匙

③ 葱花‧‧‧‧‧‧‧‧‧‧‧‧‧ 1 大匙
薑絲‧‧‧‧‧‧‧‧‧‧‧‧‧ 1 大匙
香茶‧‧‧‧‧‧‧‧‧‧‧‧‧ 1 大匙

4 eggs

① 2-1/2 c. water
3 T. pickled cucumber juice (or soy sauce)
1/2 t. salt
1 t. garlic paste
1 T. fried oil

② 1 c. broth
1/4 t. salt

③ 1 T. green onion (chopped)
1 T. shredded ginger root
1 T. coriander

❶蛋打散，加①料拌勻並除去泡沫。

❷蛋液倒入深盤中，水開以小火蒸約 12 分鐘，用牙籤試插蛋液不會流出即熟。

❸②料燒開，順盤邊倒入蒸好的蛋內，上擺③料即可。

❶ Beat eggs. Add ① and mix evenly. Remove bubbles.

❷ Pour egg mixture into deep bowl. Bring water to a boil. Steam egg mixture over low heat for about 12 minutes. Use toothpick to check consistency of egg mixture. When no liquid runs, remove from heat.

❸ Bring ② to a boil. Pour around inner edge of egg mixture bowl. Sprinkle with ③ and serve.

雙色烘蛋　TWO COLOR OMELET

4 人份　Serves 4

營養含量 Nutritional Content		
蛋白質 Protein	（公克）(g)	6
脂　肪 Fat	（公克）(g)	12
醣 Carbohydrates	（公克）(g)	2
膽固醇 Cholesterol	（毫克）(mg)	200
熱　量 Calories	（大卡）(Cal)	140

1 人份　Per Serving

　　蛋··················· 3 個
　　鹽··················· ¼ 小匙
①｛小黃瓜絲··· 75 公克（ 2 兩）
　　紅蘿蔔絲·········· 75 公克
　　葱花················· 2 大匙
②｛高湯················· 1 杯
　　醬油················· 1 小匙
　　太白粉··········· 1 ½ 小匙
　　沙拉油·············· 2 大匙

3 eggs
1/4 t. salt
2-2/3 oz. (75 g.)
　shredded gherkin
　cucumber
① 2-2/3 oz. (75 g.)
　shredded carrot
　2 T. green onions
　(chopped)
　1 c. broth
② 1 t. soy sauce
　1-1/2 t. cornstarch
　2 T. vegetable oil

❶蛋打散，加入 ¼ 小匙鹽及①料拌勻備用。

❷油 2 大匙燒熱，將鍋輕搖一下，使油遍佈鍋面，倒入蛋液，以小火煎至兩面呈金黃色取出。

❸將②料煮成薄糊狀，淋於烘蛋上即可。

❶ Beat eggs. Add 1/4 t. salt and ①. Mix well and set aside.

❷ Heat 2 T. oil in preheated wok. Spread oil evenly around by lightly shaking wok. Pour in egg mixture. Fry over low heat until two sides are golden. Remove from heat.

❸ Cook ② until slightly thickened. Pour over omelet and serve.

蔬菜類

1. 飲食中不可或缺的纖維質

蔬菜是飲食纖維的主要來源。所謂飲食纖維乃是食物中不為人類腸胃道消化酵素分解的物質，通常存在植物的細胞與細胞壁之間。它不僅會吸收水分使腸道糞體變大，同時刺激腸道蠕動，縮短糞體通過腸道的時間，使有毒物質與腸黏膜接觸減少，避免腸黏膜受侵害。此等功能可預防便秘、痔瘡、大腸癌及直腸癌等症。又因其使腸胃道吸收時間縮短，熱能吸收減少，所以較不易肥胖。同時因為飲食纖維可延緩葡萄糖進入血液，故有助於糖尿病的預防及治療。

飲食纖維也可與膽汁結合，使膽汁無法再吸收而排出體外。膽汁是脂質（包括膽固醇）及脂溶性維生素吸收所必須的物質，一旦由糞便排出增加，自然會減少膽固醇等的吸收；同時為使脂質等物質吸收正常，會刺激膽汁的再合成，而膽固醇為製造膽汁的主要原料，因而血中膽固醇量隨膽汁排泄與合成的增加而減少，即可降低罹患心血管性疾病。

飲食中糙米、全麥麵包、豆類、筍類、蔬菜（芹菜、莧菜等）、帶皮水果及未過濾的果汁等均含較多的飲食纖維，在日常飲食上應多選用以維護健康。

2. 防止甲狀腺腫大的海產植物

甲狀腺激素最主要的功能是促進新陳代謝，調節生物體的機能；而碘為甲狀腺激素的主要成份，飲食中缺乏碘會影響細胞的氧化及人體的基礎代謝（即維持體溫、消化及呼吸等不自主活動所需的能量）；而甲狀腺素為維持正常的新陳代謝功能，會使甲狀腺因工作過度而腫大。多食用含碘較多的食物，如海帶、髮菜、紫菜等海產植物，即可預防及治療腫大的甲狀腺。

3. 抵抗疾病的第一道防線～維生素 A

人體組織器官的細胞（腦除外），各有其生命週期，而且快慢不一。其中週期最短的莫過於表皮上層的黏膜細胞，只有 1～3 天的生命；故而一旦營養不足，首當其衝受損最大的就是黏膜細胞。而消化、呼吸、口及鼻等器官上的黏膜細胞是防禦細菌入侵的第一道防線，所以抵抗疾病必須要有完整的黏膜層，而維持此功能者主要是維生素 A。

維生素 A 的功能，除了增加疾病的抵抗能力與預防夜盲症及乾眼症外，還可維護皮膚的光澤，並可預防皮膚癌。飲食中維生素 A 有三分之一來自動物性食物，如牛奶、蛋、肉等；另三分之二來自維生素 A 的先質—胡蘿蔔素。所以，每日飲食中一定要有一碟富含胡蘿蔔素的深綠色、深黃、紅色類蔬菜（如菠菜、胡蘿蔔等），使黏膜細胞健全，以防禦不時入侵的細菌，免受患病之苦。

VEGETABLES

1. FIBER—AN ESSENTIAL PART OF ONE'S DIET

Vegetables are the main source of dietary fiber. So-called dietary fiber is a substance among foods which cannot be decomposed by the digestive enzymes in the gastro-intestinal tract. It normally exists in plant cells and cell walls. Dietary fiber absorbs water, which causes excrement expansion and stimulates **movement in the intestinal tract, thereby reducing the time feces requires to pass through the intestinal tract,** As a result, there is reduced contact with toxic substances and with the intestine's mucous membranes. These functions can prevent constipation, hemorrhoids, intestinal infections, and colon cancer.
Also, because fiber reduces the absorption time required in the intestines, caloric absorption is also reduced. Thus, one need not worry about gaining weight. Similarly, eating fiber can deter glucose from entering the blood, thereby helping to prevent and cure diabetes.

Dietary fiber can also combine with bile, guarding against further absorption of bile and expelling it from the body. Bile is essential for the absorption of fatty substances (including cholesterol) and fat soluble vitamins. When there is increased expellation of feces, reduced cholesterol absorption will naturally follow. Similarly, in order to allow for the regular absorption of fatty substances (etc.), fiber stimulates the formation of new bile. Furthermore, following the excretion of bile and the formation of new bile, the cholesterol volume in the blood is reduced as cholesterol serves as the main raw material required for its production. This process serves to decrease the occurrence of cardiovascular diseases caused by high cholesterol.

In the diet, unpolished rice, wholewheat bread, beans, bamboo shoots, vegetables (celery, amaranth), fruit with skin and unfiltered fruit juice all contain a high amount of dietary fiber. In order to maintain one's health, more of these foods should be consumed in one's daily diet.

2. SEA PLANTS—PREVENT BASEDOW'S DISEASE (GOITER)

The most essential function of the thyroid gland is the increase in metabolism and moderation of the body's functions. Furthermore, the main ingredient of the thyroid gland is iodine. If iodine is lacking in the diet, the body's cellular oxidation and basic metabolic rate (the energy required for such activities as maintaining body temperature, digestion, breathing, etc.) will be affected; Furthermore, the thyroid gland maintains regular metabolism, and it swells when the body works to an excessive degree. By eating more foods which contain iodine (sea plants such as seaweed, black moss, nori, etc.), one can prevent swelling of the thyroid gland.

3. VITAMIN A—THE FIRST LINE OF DEFENSE AGAINST DISEASE

The cells of the body's tissues and organs (besides those in the brain) all have their own life cycles which vary with respect to speed. Those cells which have the shortest lifespans are the epithelial cells—only one to three days. Therefore, those cells which are harmed the most by insufficient nutrition are the mucous membrane cells. Those mucous membrane cells which are located in the absorptive, digestive, and oral organs are the best line of defense against the attack of bacteria. Thus one must have complete mucous membrane layers in order to prevent against disease. Vitamin A is an essential source for the maintenance of mucous membranes.

Besides increasing immunity against disease, preventing night blindness, and xerophthalmia disease, Vitamin A also has the function of maintaining the luster of the skin and preventing skin cancer. A third of the Vitamin A in one's diet comes from animal type foods such as milk, eggs, and meat. The other two thirds come from the precursor of Vitamin A—carotene. Thus, in one's daily diet one must consume at least one dish which is rich in carotene such as dark green and dark yellow/red vegetables (spinach, carrots, etc.) In this way, one can enjoy healthy, strong mucous membrane cells, thereby guarding against bacteria and avoiding the diseases they carry.

素炒青花菜 STIR-FRIED BROCCOLI

營養含量 Nutritional Content		
蛋白質 Protein	（公克） (g)	1
脂 肪 Fat	（公克） (g)	8
醣 Carbohydrates	（公克） (g)	4
膽固醇 Cholesterol	（毫克） (mg)	0
熱 量 Calories	（大卡） (Cal)	92

1 人份　Per Serving

① 青花菜…………… 250 公克
　　　　　　（約 6 ½ 兩）
　洋菇‥100 公克（約 2 ½ 兩）
　紅蘿蔔 50 公克（約 1 ½ 兩）
　蒜末…………………… 1 小匙
② 鹽………………………… ½ 小匙
　味精…………………… ¼ 小匙
　沙拉油…………………… 2 大匙

① 1/2 lb. (250 g.) broccoli
　1/4 lb. (100 g.) button
　　mushrooms
　1-3/4 oz. (50 g.) carrots
　1 t. garlic (minced)
② 1/2 t. salt
　2 T. vegetable oil

❶ 青花菜切小朵，紅蘿蔔切片。

❷ ①料入滾水中川燙 30 秒撈出。

❸ 油 2 大匙燒熱，蒜末爆香，入①料速炒，並加②料調味即可。

❶ Cut broccoli into small bunches. Slice carrots.

❷ Add ① to boiling water and cook for 30 seconds. Remove broccoli.

❸ Heat 2 T. oil in preheated wok. Add minced garlic and stir-fry until fragrant. Add ① and quickly stir-fry. Season with 1/2 t. salt. Remove from heat and serve.

素炒海茸　STIR-FRIED SPIRAL KELP

營養含量 Nutritional Content		
蛋白質 Protein	（公克） (g)	2
脂 肪 Fat	（公克） (g)	8
醣 Carbohydrates	（公克） (g)	6
膽固醇 Cholesterol	（毫克） (mg)	0
熱 量 Calories	（大卡） (Cal)	104

1 人份　Per Serving

海茸 400 公克（約 10 ½ 兩）
① ┃薑絲⋯⋯⋯⋯⋯⋯ 1 大匙
　┃紅辣椒（切片）⋯⋯ ½ 小匙
　┃醬油⋯⋯⋯⋯⋯⋯ 1 大匙
　┃鹽⋯⋯⋯⋯⋯⋯⋯ ½ 小匙
② ┃糖⋯⋯⋯⋯⋯⋯⋯ 1 小匙
　┃醋⋯⋯⋯⋯⋯⋯⋯ 1 小匙
　┃水⋯⋯⋯⋯⋯⋯⋯ ½ 杯
　九層塔⋯⋯⋯⋯⋯⋯ 1 杯
　沙拉油⋯⋯⋯⋯⋯⋯ 2 大匙

14 oz. (400 g.) spiral
　　seaweed
① ┃1 T. shredded ginger
　┃　root
　┃1/2 t. red chili peppers
　┃　(sliced)
　┃1 T. soy sauce
　┃1/2 t. salt
② ┃1 t. sugar
　┃1 t. vinegar
　┃1/2 c. water
　1 c. fresh basil leaves
　2 T. vegetable oil

❶海茸切 5 公分長段。

❷油 2 大匙燒熱，下①料爆香，隨入海茸大火炒數下，加②料煮滾，改小火燜煮約 5 ～ 10 分鐘，下九層塔，速炒即可。

■如無九層塔可改用蒜末 1 小匙。

❶ Cut spiral seaweed into slices, 2″ long.

❷ Heat 2 T. oil in preheated wok. Add ① and quickly stir-fry until fragrant. Add spiral seaweed and stir-fry over high heat. Add ② and bring to a boil. Reduce heat and simmer for 5 to 10 minutes. Add fresh basil leaves. Stir-fry quickly and remove from heat. Serve.

■ 1 t. minced garlic may be substituted for fresh basil leaves.

干貝白菜燉 SCALLOP AND CABBAGE STEW

4 人份　Serves 4

營養含量 Nutritional Content		
蛋白質 Protein	（公克） (g)	2
脂　肪 Fat	（公克） (g)	5
醣 Carbohydrates	（公克） (g)	5
膽固醇 Cholesterol	（毫克） (mg)	8
熱　量 Calories	（大卡） (Cal)	73

1 人份　Per Serving

干貝2個‥‥ 10公克(約 ⅓兩)
大白菜‥‥‥‥‥ 400 公克
　　　　（約 10 ½ 兩）
香菇‥‥‥‥‥‥‥ 5 朵
鹽‥‥‥‥‥‥‥ ⅔ 小匙
酒‥‥‥‥‥‥‥ ½ 小匙
① 高湯(蒸干貝餘汁)‥ 2 大匙
雞油‥‥‥‥‥‥‥ 1 大匙

1/3 oz. (10 g.) 2 scallops
1 lb. (400 g.) Chinese
　cabbage (Nappa)
5 Chinese black
　mushrooms
2/3 t. salt
1/2 t. cooking wine
① 2 T. juice from steamed
　scallops
1 T. chicken fat

❶干貝加水 2 大匙，入鍋蒸軟（約 20 分鐘）撕成絲，汁留用，香菇泡軟切絲。
❷大白菜去頭部，頭尾各劃四刀，切口深約 5 公分，以滾水稍燙軟（約 3 分鐘）取出。
❸將大白菜置蒸碗中，加①料，並擺上干貝、香菇，入鍋大火蒸約 30 分鐘或以電鍋（外鍋加水 1 杯）蒸熟即可。
■如無干貝可用火腿代替。

❶ Place scallops plus 2 T. water in steamer and steam for about 20 minutes until soft . Remove and tear scallops into strips. Reserve scallop juice for later use. Soak Chinese black mushrooms until soft and slice into strips.
❷ Remove stalk of cabbage and make 4 cuts, 2'' deep, on each side. Blanch in boiling water until soft (about 3 minutes) and remove from heat.
❸ Place cabbage in bowl. Add ①. Place scallops and mushrooms on top. Place in steamer and steam over high heat for about 30 minutes (or steam in electric rice steamer with 1 c. water in outer pot).
■ Ham may be substituted for scallops.

素炒高麗菜芽
STIR-FRIED CABBAGE SPROUTS

營養含量 Nutritional Content		
蛋白質 Protein	（公克） (g)	1
脂　肪 Fat	（公克） (g)	11
醣 Carbohydrates	（公克） (g)	4
膽固醇 Cholesterol	（毫克） (mg)	0
熱　量 Calories	（大卡） (Cal)	119

1 人份　Per Serving

高麗菜芽·········· 400 公克
　　　　　　（約 10 ½ 兩）
蒜末················· 2 小匙
鹽··················· ⅓ 小匙
沙拉油·············· 3 大匙

1 lb. (400 g.) cabbage
　sprouts (or brussel
　sprouts)
2 t. garlic (minced)
1/3 t. salt
3 T. vegetable oil

❶高麗菜芽對切為二。

❷油 3 大匙燒熱，蒜末炒香，入高麗菜芽及鹽大火炒熟即可。

■高麗菜芽可改用空心菜、油菜、芥蘭菜等。

❶ Cut cabbage sprouts in two.

❷ Heat 3 T. oil in preheated wok. Stir-fry minced garlic until fragrant. Add cabbage sprouts and salt. Stir-fry over high heat until done. Serve.

■ Other green leafy vegetables may be substituted for cabbage sprouts.

金銀芽菜 GOLD AND SILVER SPROUTS

4 人份　Serves 4

營養含量 Nutritional Content		
蛋白質 Protein	（公克） (g)	2
脂　肪 Fat	（公克） (g)	8
醣 Carbohydrates	（公克） (g)	5
膽固醇 Cholesterol	（毫克） (mg)	0
熱　量 Calories	（大卡） (Cal)	100

1 人份　Per Serving

① 麵筋泡‥10公克(約 ¼ 兩)
葱(3 公分長) ……… 6 段
韭菜(3 公分長)… 20公克
　　　　　　　　(約 ½ 兩)
綠豆芽………… 400公克
　　　　　　　(約 10 ½ 兩)

② 鹽………………… ½ 小匙
糖………………… ¼ 小匙
醋………………… 1 小匙
沙拉油…………… 2 大匙

① 1/3 oz. (10 g.) gluten balls (fried)
6 sections green onion (1-1/4")
3/4 oz. (20 g.) Chinese chives, cut into 1-1/4" long
1 lb. (400 g.) mung bean sprouts

② 1/2 t. salt
1/4 t. sugar
1 t. vinegar
2 T. vegetable oil

❶麵筋泡稍拍平切成三段。

❷油 2 大匙燒熱，麵筋泡小火炒酥取出，再下①料爆香，入綠豆芽大火炒數下，加②料及麵筋泡炒均勻即可。

■如無麵筋泡可用豆包取代。

❶ Press gluten balls and cut into three sections.

❷ Heat 2 T. oil in preheated wok. Stir-fry gluten balls over low heat until crispy. Remove from heat. Stir-fry ① until fragrant. Add mung bean sprouts and stir-fry quickly over high heat. Add ② and gluten balls; stir-fry to mix. Remove from heat and serve.

■Bean curd pockets may be substituted for gluten balls.

高麗五彩捲 FIVE-COLOR CABBAGE ROLLS

營養含量 Nutritional Content		
蛋白質 Protein	（公克） (g)	3
脂　肪 Fat	（公克） (g)	9
醣 Carbohydrates	（公克） (g)	5
膽固醇 Cholesterol	（毫克） (mg)	0
熱　量 Calories	（大卡） (Cal)	113

1 人份　Per Serving

高麗菜葉‥‥‥‥‥ 200 公克
　　　　　　　（約 5 ½ 兩）
薑絲‥‥‥‥‥‥‥‥ 1 大匙
① { 豆干絲‥ 30 公克（約 1 兩）
　 木耳絲‥‥ 75 公克（2 兩）
　 小黃瓜絲‥‥‥‥‥ 75 公克
　 紅蘿蔔絲‥‥‥‥‥ 50 公克
　　　　　　　（約 1 ½ 兩）
② { 醬油膏‥‥‥‥‥‥ 1 大匙
　 糖‥‥‥‥‥‥‥‥ 1 小匙
　 白醋‥‥‥‥‥‥‥ 1 大匙
　 麻油‥‥‥‥‥‥ ½ 小匙
　 葱末或薑末‥‥‥‥ 1 大匙
　 冷開水‥‥‥‥‥‥ 1 大匙
　 沙拉油‥‥‥‥‥‥ 2 大匙

❶ 高麗菜葉燙軟（約 2 分鐘），油 2 大匙燒熱，薑絲爆香，入①料大火速炒 30 秒取出。②料調勻為沾料。

❷ 每一高麗菜葉包一份①料，捲成圓筒狀，依次捲好切成 3 公分長段排盤，食時淋上②料即可。

1/2 lb. (200 g.)
　cabbage leaves
1 T. shredded ginger
　root
① { 1 oz. (30 g.) pressed
　　bean curd, shredded
　2-2/3 oz. (75 g.) shredded
　　wood ear
　2-2/3 oz. (75 g.) shredded
　　gherkin cucumber
　1-3/4 oz. (50 g.)
　　shredded carrot
② { 1 T. soy sauce paste
　1 t. sugar
　1 T. white vinegar
　1/2 t. sesame oil
　1 T. green onion or
　　ginger root (minced)
　1 T. cold water
　2 T. vegetable oil

❶ Boil cabbage leaves for about 2 minutes until done. Heat 2 T. oil in preheated wok. Stir-fry ginger until fragrant. Add ① and stir-fry over high heat for 30 seconds. Remove from heat. Mix ② evenly and set aside.

❷ Place one portion of ① on cabbage leaf; roll up leaf into cylinder. Continue to make rest of cabbage rolls. Cut rolls into sections, 1-/4″ long. Arrange rolls on serving plate. Before serving, pour ② over rolls.

凉拌蘆筍 ASPARAGUS SALAD

營養含量 Nutritional Content		
蛋白質 Protein	（公克） (g)	1
脂　肪 Fat	（公克） (g)	4
醣 Carbohydrates	（公克） (g)	8
膽固醇 Cholesterol	（毫克） (mg)	0
熱　量 Calories	（大卡） (Cal)	72

1 人份　Per Serving

蘆筍（去老皮）‥ 400 公克
（約 10 ½ 兩）
① ⎰ 鹽………………… ½ 小匙
　 ⎱ 水………………… 6 杯
　 ⎧ 沙拉油…………… 1 大匙
　 ⎪ 糖………………… 1 大匙
② ⎨ 醋………………… 2 大匙
　 ⎪ 鹽………………… ½ 小匙
　 ⎩ 胡椒……………… ⅛ 小匙
③ ⎰ 靑椒末…………… 2 大匙
　 ⎱ 洋葱末…………… 2 大匙

1 lb. (400 g.) asparagus
　 (stalks peeled)
① ⎰ 1/2 t. salt
　 ⎱ 6 c. water
　 ⎧ 1 T. vegetable oil
　 ⎪ 1 T. sugar
② ⎨ 2 T. vinegar
　 ⎪ 1/2 t. salt
　 ⎩ 1/8 t. pepper
③ ⎰ 2 T. green pepper
　 ⎪ 　 (minced)
　 ⎱ 2 T. onion (minced)

❶蘆筍切段，入煮開的①料中大火煮熟（約2分鐘）取出。

❷②料調勻，入蘆筍及③料拌勻置盤即可。

■夏天冰涼食用更佳。

■可以紅蘿蔔、巴西利彩盤。

❶ Cut asparagus into sections. Bring ① to a boil; add asparagus and cook over high heat for 2 minutes or until done. Remove.

❷ Mix ② ; Pour over asparagus and ③ ; mix well and serve.

■ This dish is especially good during the summer when served chilled.

■ Carrot and parsley may be used as garnish.

鮮磨菜心　MUSHROOM AND BOK CHOY

營養含量 Nutritional Content		
蛋白質 Protein	（公克） (g)	1
脂　肪 Fat	（公克） (g)	8
醣 Carbohydrates	（公克） (g)	4
膽固醇 Cholesterol	（毫克） (mg)	6
熱　量 Calories	（大卡） (Cal)	92

1 人份　Per Serving

洋菇‥200 公克(約 5 ½ 兩)
青江菜(小棵)‥‥ 200 公克
① { 水‥‥‥‥‥‥‥‥ 6 杯
　　鹽‥‥‥‥‥‥‥‥ 1 小匙
② { 高湯‥‥‥‥‥‥‥ 1 杯
　　鹽‥‥‥‥‥‥‥‥ ¼ 小匙
　　味精‥‥‥‥‥‥‥ ⅓ 小匙
　　雞油(或熟油)‥‥‥ 2 大匙
③ { 太白粉‥‥‥‥‥‥ 1 ½ 小匙
　　水‥‥‥‥‥‥‥‥ 1 大匙

1/2 lb. (200 g.) button
　　mushrooms
1/2 lb. (200 g.) small bok
　　choy
① { 6 c. water
　　1 t. salt
② { 1 c. broth
　　1/4 t. salt
　　2 T. chicken fat　(or
　　　fried oil)
③ { 1-1/2 t. cornstarch } mix
　　1 T. water

❶青江菜切半備用。
❷①料煮開，入洋菇，青江菜分別燙熟即刻撈出擺盤上。
❸將②料燒開，並以③料勾芡，淋於菜上即可。

❶ Cut bok choy in half and set aside.
❷ Bring ① to a boil. Blanch button mushrooms and bok choy separately in boiling water and remove immediately. Place on serving plate.
❸ Bring ② to a boil. Thicken with ③. Pour over vegetables and serve.

銀魚燴芥菜 SILVERFISH AND MUSTARD CABBAGE

營養含量 Nutritional Content		
蛋白質 Protein	（公克） (g)	2
脂　肪 Fat	（公克） (g)	9
醣 Carbohydrates	（公克） (g)	4
膽固醇 Cholesterol	（毫克） (mg)	4
熱　量 Calories	（大卡） (Cal)	105

1 人份　Per Serving

芥菜心‥‥‥‥‥‥ 400 公克
　　　　　　（約 10 ½ 兩）
銀魚（魩仔魚）‥‥‥ 20 公克
　　　　　　（約 ½ 兩）
① { 水‥‥‥‥‥‥‥‥ 6 杯
　　鹽‥‥‥‥‥‥‥‥ ½ 小匙
　　薑絲‥‥‥‥‥‥‥ 1 大匙
② { 酒‥‥‥‥‥‥‥‥ ½ 小匙
　　高湯‥‥‥‥‥‥‥ 1 杯
　　鹽‥‥‥‥‥‥‥‥ ½ 小匙
③ { 太白粉‥‥‥‥‥‥ 1 ½ 小匙
　　水‥‥‥‥‥‥‥‥ 1 大匙
　　沙拉油‥‥‥‥‥‥ 2 大匙

14 oz. (400 g.) mustard
　　cabbage, cut off
　　leaves
3/4 oz. (20 g.) silverfish
① { 6 c. water
　　1/2 t. salt
　　1 T. shredded ginger
　　　root
② { 1/2 t. cooking wine
　　1 c. broth
　　1/2 t. salt
③ { 1-1/2 t. cornstarch } mix
　　1 T. water
2 T. vegetable oil

❶芥菜心切 5 公分長段備用。

❷將①料煮開，入芥菜煮滾 2 分鐘撈出。

❸油 2 大匙燒熱，薑絲爆香，入②料煮開，隨入銀魚及芥菜待滾改小火煮 3 分鐘，以③料勾芡即可盛盤。

❶ Cut cabbage into 2″ long sections and set aside.

❷ Bring ① to a boil. Add mustard cabbage and boil for 2 minutes. Remove from heat with slotted spoon.

❸ Heat 2 T. oil in preheated wok. Quickly stir-fry ginger until fragrant. Add ② and bring to a boil. Add silverfish and mustard cabbage. Bring to another boil. Reduce heat and simmer for 3 minutes. Thicken with ③, remove and serve.

肉末茄子香 EGGPLANT AND GROUND PORK

4 人份　Serves 4

營養含量 Nutritional Content		
蛋白質 Protein	（公克） (g)	3
脂　肪 Fat	（公克） (g)	9
醣 Carbohydrates	（公克） (g)	3
膽固醇 Cholesterol	（毫克） (mg)	8
熱　量 Calories	（大卡） (Cal)	105

1 人份　Per Serving

茄子……… 300 公克（ 8 兩）
絞肉… 50 公克（約 1½ 兩）
蒜末………………… 2 大匙
九層塔………………… ½ 杯
① 鹽………………… ½ 小匙
糖………………… ½ 小匙
醋………………… ½ 小匙
太白粉…………… ½ 小匙
水………………… 3 大匙
沙拉油……………… 3 杯

2/3 lb. (300 g.) eggplant
1-3/4 oz. (50 g.) ground
　pork
2 T. garlic (minced)
1/2 c. fresh basil leaves
① 1/2 t. salt
1/2 t. sugar
1/2 t. vinegar
1/2 t. cornstarch
3 T. water   } mix
3 c. vegetable oil

❶茄子切約 6 公分長段，再對剖成四長條。

❷油燒熱，把茄子中火炸軟（約 2 分鐘）取出，留油 1 大匙，將絞肉略炒，隨入蒜末炒香，再入茄子、九層塔及①料炒勻即可。

■茄子以油炸軟，色香味較佳，蒸軟亦可。

❶ Cut eggplant into sections, 2-1/4" long. Cut each section lengthwise in fourth.

❷ Heat 3 c. oil in preheated wok. Deep-fry eggplant over medium heat for about 2 minutes or until soft. Remove eggplant, leaving 1 T. oil in wok. Slightly stir-fry ground pork . Add minced garlic and stir-fry until fragrant. Add eggplant, fresh basil leaves, and ①; stir-fry to mix. Remove from heat and serve.

■ Eggplant may be either cooked in boiling water or deep-fried until soft. Deep-fried eggplant is more flavorful, colorful and fragrant.

蠔油包生菜 LETTUCE IN OYSTER SAUCE

營養含量 Nutritional Content		
蛋白質　　（公克） Protein　　　（g）		1
脂　肪　　（公克） Fat　　　　　（g）		8
醣　　　　（公克） Carbohydrates （g）		4
膽固醇　　（毫克） Cholesterol　（mg）		—
熱　量　　（大卡） Calories　　（Cal）		92

1 人份　Per Serving

包生菜············· 400 公克
　　　　　　（約 10 ½ 兩）
蒜末················· 1 小匙
①⎰ 蠔油··············· 1 ½ 大匙
　 醬油··············· 2 小匙
　 酒················· 1 小匙
　 糖················· ½ 小匙
　 麻油··············· ½ 小匙
　 太白粉············· 1 ½ 小匙
　 水················· 5 大匙
　 沙拉油············· 2 大匙

1 lb. (400 g.) lettuce
1 t. garlic (minced)
⎰ 1-1/2 T. oyster sauce
　 2 t. soy sauce
　 1 t. cooking wine
①⎰ 1/2 t. sugar
　 1/2 t. sesame oil
　 1-1/2 t. cornstarch
　 5 T. water
2 T. vegetable oil

❶包生菜切大片備用。

❷油 2 大匙燒熱，蒜末爆香，再下包生菜大火炒熟取出置盤內。

❸①料煮滾，淋於包生菜上即可。

❶ Cut lettuce into large slices and set aside.

❷ Heat 2 T. oil in preheated wok. Stir-fry minced garlic until fragrant. Add lettuce and stir-fry over high heat until done. Remove from heat and place on serving plate.

❸ Bring ① to a boil. Pour over lettuce and serve.

什錦蒟蒻 COLORFUL KONNYAKU

營養含量 Nutritional Content		
蛋白質 Protein	（公克）(g)	1
脂肪 Fat	（公克）(g)	8
醣 Carbohydrates	（公克）(g)	2
膽固醇 Cholesterol	（毫克）(mg)	—
熱量 Calories	（大卡）(Cal)	84

1 人份　Per Serving

蒟蒻 1 塊‥150 公克（ 4 兩）
香菇…………………… 3 朵
葱(3 公分長)……… 6 段
① {
水……………………… ½ 杯
醬油………………… 1 大匙
糖………………… ¼ 小匙
鹽………………… ¼ 小匙
味精……………… ¼ 小匙
}
② {
熟筍片………… 100 公克
（約 2 ½ 兩）
豌豆莢 50 公克（約 1 ½ 兩）
熟紅蘿蔔………… 50 公克
}
③ {
太白粉…………… 1 小匙
水……………… 1 大匙
}
沙拉油…………… 2 大匙

1/3 lb. (150 g.) 1 piece
of konnyaku
3 Chinese black
mushrooms
6 sections green onions
(1-1/4″)
① {
1/2 c. water
1 T. soy sauce
1/4 t. sugar
1/4 t. salt
}
② {
3-1/2 oz. (100 g.)
bamboo shoots
(cooked slices)
1-3/4 oz. (50 g.) carrots
(cooked slices)
1-3/4 oz. (50 g.) Chinese
pea pods
}
③ { 1 t. cornstarch
1 T. water } mix
2 T. vegetable oil

❶蒟蒻切 0.5 公分薄片，每片中間切一裂口，再將蒟蒻片由中間翻轉，即成麻花形，以滾水川燙 1 分鐘取出，香菇泡軟切塊備用。

❷油 2 大匙燒熱，炒香葱段，加①料及蒟蒻煮開後改小火煮 5 分鐘，再下②料煮滾，以③料勾芡即可。

❶ Slice konnyaku into pieces, 1/4″ thick. Cut slit down middle of each piece. Turn one end of each piece inside out from slit. Boil for 1 minute. Remove and drain. Soak mushrooms until soft, cut into pieces and set aside.

❷ Heat 2 T. oil in preheated wok. Stir-fry green onion sections until fragrant. Add ① and konnyaku. Bring to a boil. Reduce heat and simmer for 5 minutes. Add ② and bring to another boil. Thicken with ③ and serve.

燴蠶豆筍丁
LIMA BEANS AND BAMBOO SHOOT CUBES

4 人份　Serves 4

營養含量 Nutritional Content		
蛋白質 　　（公克） Protein 　　　（g）	3
脂　肪 　　（公克） Fat 　　　　　（g）	9
醣　　　　（公克） Carbohydrates （g）	3
膽固醇 　　（毫克） Cholesterol （mg）	8
熱　量 　　（大卡） Calories 　　（Cal）	105

1 人份　Per Serving

嫩蠶豆…………… 100 公克
筍丁‥100 公克（約 2½ 兩）
火腿…… 40 公克（約 1 兩）
① { 薑末………………… 1 小匙
　　 蒜末………………… 1 小匙
② { 酒………………… ½ 大匙
　　 水………………… ½ 杯
　　 糖………………… ½ 小匙
③ { 水………………… 2 大匙
　　 太白粉………… 2 小匙
沙拉油…………… 2 大匙

1/4 lb. (100 g.) lima
　beans
1/4 lb. (100 g.) bamboo
　shoot (cubes)
1-1/2 oz. (40 g.) ham
① { 1 t. ginger root
　　　(minced)
　　 1 t. garlic (minced)
② { 1/2 T. cooking wine
　　 1/2 c. water
　　 1/2 t. sugar
③ { 2 T. water
　　 2 t. cornstarch } mix
2 T. vegetable oil

❶筍煮熟切丁，火腿蒸熟切 1 公分四方薄片。

❷油燒熱，將①料爆香，入火腿、筍丁、蠶豆炒數下，隨入②料煮開，改小火再煮約 3 分鐘，以③料勾芡即可。

■如無火腿，可用肉丁取代。

❶ Cook bamboo shoots until done. Steam ham until done and cut into slices, 1/2" x 1/2".

❷ Heat 2 T. oil in preheated wok. Add ① and stir-fry until fragrant. Add ham, bamboo shoot cubes, and lima beans; stir to mix. Add ② and bring to a boil. Reduce heat and simmer for 3 minutes. Thicken with ③ and serve.

■Beef or pork cubes may be substituted for ham.

紅燒蒟蒻

SOY-SIMMERED KONNYAKU

營養含量 Nutritional Content		
蛋白質 Protein	（公克） (g)	3
脂　肪 Fat	（公克） (g)	9
醣 Carbohydrates	（公克） (g)	5
膽固醇 Cholesterol	（毫克） (mg)	0
熱　量 Calories	（大卡） (Cal)	113

1 人份　Per Serving

① 蒟蒻⋯⋯⋯ 150 公克（4 兩）
油炸烤麩 40 公克（約 1 兩）
筍⋯⋯ 100 公克（約 2½ 兩）
紅蘿蔔⋯⋯⋯⋯⋯ 100 公克
（約 2½ 兩）

② 小香菇（泡軟）⋯⋯⋯⋯ 5 朵
薑⋯⋯⋯⋯⋯⋯⋯⋯ 3 片

③ 醬油⋯⋯⋯⋯⋯⋯ 3 大匙
糖⋯⋯⋯⋯⋯⋯⋯ 2 小匙
海山醬或番茄醬⋯⋯ ½ 大匙
麻油⋯⋯⋯⋯⋯⋯ ½ 小匙
水⋯⋯⋯⋯⋯⋯⋯⋯ 2 杯
沙拉油⋯⋯⋯⋯⋯⋯ 2 大匙

① 1/3 lb. (150 g.) konnyaku
1-1/3 oz. (40 g.) deep-fried bran puffs (kaofu)
1/4 lb. (100 g.) bamboo shoots
1/4 lb. (100 g.) carrots

② 5 Chinese black mushrooms (soaked)
3 slices ginger root

③ 3 T. soy sauce
2 t. sugar
1/2 T. hoisin sauce (or ketchup)
1/2 t. sesame oil
2 c. water
2 T. vegetable oil

❶ 蒟蒻切片，做成麻花形（做法參考第 115 頁）以滾水川燙 1 分鐘取出，每塊烤麩切成 4 片，筍、紅蘿蔔切滾刀塊備用。

❷ 油燒熱，將②料爆香，下①料炒數下，隨入③料以大火煮滾，改以小火燜煮約 30 分鐘至汁將乾即可。

■ 可以巴西利點綴。

❶ Slice konnyaku and turn one side of each inside-out (refer to page 115 for directions). Boil for 1 minute and remove from heat. Cut each piece of kaofu into 4 slices. Cut bamboo shoots and carrots into pieces. Set aside.

❷ Heat 2 T. oil in preheated wok. Add ② and stir-fry until fragrant. Add ① and quickly stir-fry. Add ③ and bring to a boil over high heat. Reduce heat and simmer for 30 minutes or until liquid is almost absorbed. Serve.

■ Parsley may be used as garnish.

蔬菜沙拉 VEGETABLE SALAD

營養含量 Nutritional Content		
蛋白質 Protein	（公克） (g)	1
脂 肪 Fat	（公克） (g)	6
醣 Carbohydrates	（公克） (g)	6
膽固醇 Cholesterol	（毫克） (mg)	0
熱 量 Calories	（大卡） (Cal)	82

1 人份　Per Serving

包生菜…………… 200 公克
　　　　　　（約 5 ½ 兩）
番茄…… 80 公克（約 2 兩）
小黃瓜 60 公克（約 1 ½ 兩）
青椒…… 30 公克（約 1 兩）
洋蔥………………… 30 公克
① { 沙拉油………… 1 ½ 大匙
鹽………………… ¼ 小匙
檸檬汁………… 2 大匙
蜂蜜………………… 2 小匙
櫻桃（切碎）……… 1 大匙

1/2 lb. (200 g.) lettuce
2-3/4 oz. (80 g.) tomatoes
2 oz. (60 g.) gherkin
　cucumbers
1 oz. (30 g.) green
　pepper
1 oz. (30 g.) onion
① { 1-1/2 T. vegetable oil
1/4 t. salt
2 T. lemon juice
2 t. honey
1 T. cherries (minced)

❶包生菜、番茄切塊，小黃瓜切片，青椒、洋蔥切環片，①料拌勻備用。
❷將所有材料置盤上，食時淋上①料即可食用。
■夏天如冰涼，食用味更佳。

❶ Cut lettuce and tomatoes into chunks. Slice gherkin cucumbers. Slice green pepper and onions into rings. Mix together ① and set aside.
❷ Place all vegetables on serving plate. Pour ① over vegetables and serve.
■ This dish is especially good during the summer when served chilled.

水果類 FRUITS

水果是供給飲食纖維（詳見蔬菜篇）、維生素及礦物質的良好來源。

1. 維持血管壁彈性的維生素 C

維生素 C 是細胞的黏著劑、能幫助膠原蛋白的形成。膠原蛋白是所有結締組織的主要成份，也是皮膚、軟骨、牙齒、疤痕組織及骨骼的成份之一。因此，維生素 C 不僅可使血管壁強韌而有伸縮性，血液循環順暢，還能使骨骼堅實而具活力，皮膚完整而有彈性，肌肉結實而柔韌，並具有協助殺滅微生物的能力；缺乏維生素 C 則有皮下出血、牙齒脫落、骨骼脆弱不堅、傷口不易癒合、抗病能力減低等現象。

所以每日應攝取含有維生素 C 的食物，而其中含量較多的有蕃石榴、柑橘、柳丁、葡萄柚、番茄等水果。

2. 幫助消化及維持神經傳遞正常的維生素 B 羣與礦物質

維生素 B 羣及礦物質是幫助消化的主要成份，同時也是刺激神經衝動，使其傳遞正常所需的物質。這些物質必須齊全才能發揮功效，缺乏任何一種，都會使功能受阻，產生身體異常的現象。

水果和蔬菜是維生素及礦物質的來源，正好彌補五穀及肉類的不足。每日飲食均衡攝取，則各營養素不虞匱乏，腸胃消化的功能及神經傳遞的運作將正常無礙。

3. 如何預防貧血

引起貧血的原因很多，單以營養素的缺乏來說，其中之一乃是血紅素的主要成份─鐵質及蛋白質缺失所造成。因為飲食攝取的偏失，較少選用含鐵質的食物，加上其吸收率低（只有 10 ～ 30 ％）；而且飲食型態也會影響其吸收，譬如有維生素 C 及肉類的存在，其吸收率增加五倍以上；若有鹼性物質或飲食纖維攝取過量，則會干擾鐵質的吸收。為避免貧血的產生，除應攝取含鐵質較多的食物外，還須注意飲食中要有維生素 C 及肉類的存在。食物中鐵質來源以肝臟、牡蠣最為豐富，但該二種食物甚少出現在菜餚上，因此，其主要來源是乾果類（如黑棗、杏子、葡萄乾等）的補充，其次是深色肉類（如牛、羊肉），這些食物均有助於預防因鐵質缺乏而造成的貧血。

1. VITAMIN C—MAINTAINS THE ELASTICITY OF THE BLOOD VESSEL WALLS

Fruits provide a fine source of dietary fiber (please refer to vegetable section), vitamins, and minerals. Vitamin C is an intercellular substance which can help the formation of collagen. Collagen is the major ingredient of all connective tissues as well as of the skin, cartilage, teeth, scar tissue, and bone matrices.Therefore, Vitamin C is not only able to strengthen the blood vessel walls but also allows for elasticity and smooth blood circulation. Vitamin C can also make the body frame solid and full of vitality, the skin healthy and flexible, the muscles durable but pliable. Furthermore, Vitamin C helps eliminate the harmful capabilities of micro- organisms. Vitamin C deficiency results in hemorrhaging under the skin, teeth loss, skeletal tenderness, uneasily healed wounds, and a reduction of resistance to disease, etc.

Thus one must consume food which contains Vitamin C on a daily basis. Those foods which contain the highest concentrations of Vitamin C are fruits such as oranges, tangarines, grapefruits, tomatoes, etc.

2. VITAMIN B COMPLEX AND MINERALS—HELP DIGESTION AND MAINTAIN NORMAL NERVE TRANSMISSION

Vitamin B complex and minerals are the major ingredients which aid digestion and stimulate nerve impulses required for normal transmission. These substances must be complete in order to operate most effectively. If any one type is deficient, the functions will be obstructed, thereby producing abnormal health conditions.

Fruits and vegetables are the sources of vitamins and minerals which supplement the insufficiency of grains and meats. One should have a balanced daily intake of these so that one need not worry about inadequate absorption of various nutrients and so that the normal functions of digestion and nerve transmission remain unhindered.

3. ANEMIA PREVENTION

There are many reasons for the onset of anemia. However, speaking only in terms of nutrient deficiency, the lack of iron and protein, which are essential in the production of hemoglobin, is a major cause. An imbalanced diet, whereby foods which contain iron are less frequently selected, plus iron's low absorbancy rate (only 10-30%) are factors which both contribute to anemia. Furthermore, consumption methods can also influence the level of absorption. For example, the existence of Vitamin C and meats in the diet can increase the rate of absorption by at least five times. Yet if an excessive amount of alkaline substances or edible fiber is consumed, the absorption of iron will be greatly reduced.

In order to avoid the development of anemia, besides consuming more foods which contain iron, one must also stress the inclusion of Vitamin C and meat in one's diet. Those foods which contain the richest iron source are liver and oysters, yet these two types rarely appear in the average diet. Therefore, iron intake is mainly supplemented by dried fruit (such as black dates, apricots, raisins, etc.), followed by red meats. These foods will all help prevent anemia caused by iron deficiency.

附錄 APPENDIXES
食物代換表 FOOD SUBSTITUTION/EXCHANGE TABLE

肉、魚、豆、蛋類
（每份含蛋白質 7 公克，脂肪 50 公克，熱能 73 大卡）

名　　　　稱	可食部份 生重(公克)	可食部份 熟重(公克)
肉類：畜肉/豬、牛、羊肉	35	30
禽肉/雞、鴨、鵝	35	30
內臟/豬心、豬肝、豬腰等	40	30
西式火腿	30	
肉鬆、肉乾		15
魚類：魚翅、干貝、小魚干	10	
魚肉	35	30
烏賊、槍烏賊（小管）	45	30
螃蟹、龍蝦、大蝦、蝦仁等	45	30
鮮干貝	60	
蛤蜊肉、蚵仔	75	40
海參	100	90
豆類：豆腐		100
黃豆干		70
干絲、百葉、濕豆包		25
素雞		50
豆漿		240 c.c.
蛋類：蛋（約1個）	50	

五穀根莖類
（每份含蛋白質8公克，醣類60公克，熱能272大卡）

名　　　　稱	份　　量	重量(公克)
飯	1 碗	200
稀飯	2 碗	1000
麵條（熟）、油麵	2 碗	200
乾麵條		80
乾米粉		100
吐司麵包	4 片	100
漢堡麵包	2 個	100
小餐包	4 個	100
饅頭（中型）	1 個	120
蘇打餅干	10～12 片	80
馬鈴薯（生、去皮）		360
蕃薯（生、去皮）		240
玉米（生、連心）		320
乾豆類（紅豆、綠豆等）		80
燒餅	2 個	120
爆米花（不加奶油）		60
麥片	8 大匙	80

Meat, Fish, Beans, and Eggs
(each serving contains 7 g. protein, 5 g, fat, 73 calories)

Ingredient	Weight at Purchase		Net Wt. of Edible Portion	
	oz.	g.	oz.	g.
Meats: livestock-pork, beef, mutton	1-1/4	35	1	30
poultry-chicken, duck, goose	1-1/4	35	1	30
viscera, pig's heart, pig liver, pig kidneys, etc.	1-1/2	40	1	30
western ham	1	30		
shredded pork, meat jerk			1/2	15
Fish: shark's fin, scallop, dried anchovies	1/3	10		
fish meat	1-1/4	35	1	30
squid, crab, lobster, jumbo shrimp, shrimp	1-1/3	45	1	30
fresh scallops	2-1/4	60		
clams, oysters	2-2/3	75	1-1/2	40
sea cucumber	3-1/2	100	3-1/4	90
Beans: bean curd			3-1/2	100
pressed bean curd			2-1/2	70
bean curd noodles, bean curd sheets, bean curd pockets			1	25
vegetarian chicken			1-3/4	50
soybean milk				240 c.c.
Eggs: (about one egg)			1-3/4	50

Grains and Rootstocks
(each serving contains 8 g. protein, 60 g. carbohydrates, and 272 calories)

Ingredient	Serving Amount	Weight	
		oz.	g.
Rice	1 bowl	7	200
Congee	2 bowls	2-1/4 1b	1000
Noodles	2 bowls	7	200
Dry noodles		2-3/4	80
Dried rice-flour		3-1/2	100
Toast	4 slices	3-1/2	100
Hamburger rolls	2 rolls	3-1/2	100
Small roll	4 rolls	3-1/2	100
Medium Man Tou (Chinese steamed bread)	1 man tou	4-1/4	120
Soda cracker	10-12 crackers	2-3/4	80
Potato (raw, peeled)		12-3/4	360
Sweet potato (raw, peeled)		8-1/2	240
Corn (raw, on the cob)		11-1/2	320
Dried beans (Red beans, Mung beans, etc.)		2-3/4	80
Flaky sesame flat bread (shao bing)	2 rolls	4-1/4	120
Popcorn (without butter)		2-1/4	60
Oatmeal (rolled oats)	8 tablespoons	2-3/4	80

水果類

（每份含醣類 10 公克，熱能 40 大卡）

名　　　稱	購買量 （公克）	可食量 （公克）
紅西瓜（連皮）	310	190
香瓜	200	150
＊葡萄柚	170	110
＊楊桃	170	140
蓮霧	155	130
＊柑橘類	150	110
鳳梨	150	90
＊木瓜	125	90
水梨	120	90
蘋果	100	80
葡萄	100	80
＊荔枝	100	60
芒果	90	60
李子	80	70
＊蕃石榴	60	60
香蕉	65	40
＊草莓	120	120
櫻桃（新鮮約 15 個）	110	90
桃子	125	100

1. 水果以選用新鮮者爲宜，少採用果汁
2. ＊表示維生素 C 含量較高的水果

Fruits

(each serving contains 10 g. carbohydrates, 40 calories)

Ingredient	Weight at Purchase		Net Wt. of Edible Portion	
	oz.	g.	oz.	g.
Red watermelon (with rind)	11	310	6-3/4	190
Cantaloupe	7-1/4	200	5-1/3	150
＊Grapefruit	6	170	4	110
＊Starfruit (carambola)	6	170	5	140
Wax apple	5-1/2	155	4-2/3	130
＊Citrus	5-1/3	150	4-2/3	130
Pineapple	5-1/3	150	3-1/4	90
＊Papaya	4-1/2	125	3-1/4	90
Pear	4-1/4	120	3-1/4	90
Apple	3-1/2	100	2-3/4	80
Grape	3-1/2	100	2-3/4	80
＊Lichee	3-1/2	100	2-1/4	60
Mango	3-1/4	90	2-1/4	60
Plum	2-3/4	80	2-1/2	70
＊Guava	2-1/4	60	2-1/4	60
Banana	2-1/3	65	1-1/2	40
＊Strawberry	4-1/2	120	4-1/4	120
Cherry (fresh, approx. 15)	4	110	3-1/4	90
Peach	4-1/2	125	3-1/2	100

1. It's better to use seasonal fresh fruits than fruit juice.
2. ＊ Marks those fruits which contain a higher volume of Vitamin C.

熱能營養素攝取量之計算方法

HOW TO CALCULATE THE ABSORPTION VOLUME OF CALORIES CONTAINED IN NUTRIENTS

熱能的分配

營　養　素	應佔總熱能 百　分　比	每公克所供 應的熱能
蛋　白　質	10 ～ 15 %	4 卡／公克
醣　　　類	55 ～ 60 %	4 卡／公克
脂　　　肪	20 ～ 30 %	9 卡／公克

Caloric distribution

Nutrient	Percentage Of Total Required Caloric Intake	Calories Supplied per g.
protein	10-15%	4 cal./g.
carbohydrates	55-60%	4 cal./g.
fat	20-30%	9 cal./g.

茲舉男士 35 歲輕度工作者，熱能需要量爲2,300卡（參考第 10 頁成人每日熱能建議攝取量），其食物中熱能營養素所應攝取量之計算方法如下：

公式：本身需要之熱能卡數×攝取量應佔總熱能百分比÷每公克所供應的熱能＝實際需要量

蛋白質 2,300 × 15 %÷ 4 = 86（公克）醣類 2,300 × 55 %÷ 4 = 316（公克）脂肪 2,300 × 30 %÷ 9 = 77（公克）　由上面計算得知熱能需要量爲 2300 卡者，蛋白質攝取量爲 86 公克，醣類 316 公克，脂肪 77 公克。

For example, the daily caloric requirement of 35 yr. old males who have a low level of daily physical exertion is 2,300 (refer suggested daily coloric intake for adults on page 10). You can use the following method to calculate the calories contained in the nutrients you consume according to this example.

Formula: Amount of required calories x percentage of total required caloric intake divided by calories supplied per gram = actual required amount

Protein 2,300 x 15% ÷ 4 = 86 g.　Carbohydrates 2,300 x 55% ÷ 4 = 316 g.　Fat 2,300 x 30% ÷ 9 = 77 g.

According to the above calculation, the required caloric intake for a person whose daily caloric allowance is 2300 is listed as follows: 86 g. protein 316 g. carbohydrates, 77 g. fat

維生素的功能及來源

營養素分類	功用	食物來源
維生素	維生素又稱維他命，其中能溶解於脂肪者稱脂溶性維生素，能溶解於水者稱水溶性維生素。大多數不能從身體中製造，而必需從食物中攝取，其在身體中的作用，就好像機械中的潤滑油。茲將其功用及食物來源分述如下：	
1. 脂溶性維生素 維生素 A	(1)使眼睛適應光線之變化，維持在黑暗光線下的正常視力。 (2)保護表皮、黏膜使細菌不易侵害（增加抵抗傳染病的能力）。 (3)促進牙齒和骨骼的正常生長。	肝、蛋黃、牛奶、乳酪、人造奶油、黃綠色蔬菜、水果（如青江白菜、胡蘿蔔、菠菜、番茄、木瓜、芒果等）、魚肝油、黃紅心蕃薯。
維生素 D	(1)協助鈣、磷的吸收與運用。 (2)幫助骨骼和牙齒的正常發育。 (3)為神經、肌肉正常生理上所必需。	魚肝油、蛋黃、乳酪、魚類、肝、添加維生素 D 之牛奶等。
維生素 E	(1)減少維生素 A 及多元不飽和脂肪酸的氧化，控制細胞氧化。 (2)維持動物生殖機能	穀類、米糠油、小麥胚芽油、棉子油、綠葉蔬菜、蛋黃、堅果類。
維生素 K	構成凝血酶元所必需的一種物質，可促進血液在傷口凝固，以免流血不止。	綠葉蔬菜如菠菜、萵苣是維生素 K 最好的來源，蛋黃、肝臟亦含有少量。
2. 水溶性維生素 維生素 B_1	(1)增加食慾。 (2)促進胃腸蠕動及消化液的分泌。 (3)預防及治療腳氣病、神經炎。 (4)促進動物生長。 (5)醣類的氧化作用。	胚芽米、麥芽、米糠、肝、瘦肉、酵母、豆類、蛋黃、魚卵、蔬菜等。
維生素 B_2	(1)輔助細胞的氧化還原作用。 (2)防治眼血管充血及嘴角裂痛。	酵母、內臟類、牛奶、蛋類、花生、豆類、綠葉菜、瘦肉等。
維生素 B_6	(1)為一種輔助酵素，幫助胺基酸之合成與分解。 (2)幫助色胺酸變成菸鹼酸。	肉類、魚類、蔬菜類、酵母、麥芽、肝、腎、糙米、蛋、牛奶、豆類、花生等。
維生素 B_{12}	(1)促進核酸之合成。 (2)對醣類和脂肪代謝有重要功用，並影響血液中麩基胺硫的濃度。 (3)治惡性貧血及惡性貧血神經系統的病症。	肝、腎、瘦肉、乳、乾酪、蛋等。
菸鹼酸	(1)構成醣類分解過程中二種輔助酵素的主要成分，此輔助酵素主要作用為輸送氧。 (2)使皮膚健康，也有益於神經系統的健康。	肝、酵母、糙米、全穀製品、瘦肉、蛋、魚類、乾豆類、綠葉蔬菜、牛奶等。
葉酸	(1)幫助血液的形成，可防治惡性貧血症。 (2)促成核酸及核蛋白合成。	新鮮的綠色蔬菜、肝、腎、瘦肉等。
維生素 C	(1)細胞間質的主要構成物質，使細胞間保持良好狀況。 (2)加速傷口之癒合。 (3)增加對傳染病的抵抗力。	深綠及黃紅色蔬菜、水果（如青辣椒、蕃石榴、柑橘類、番茄、檸檬等）。

VITAMINS: THEIR FUNCTIONS AND FOOD SOURCES

Vitamins	Functions	Food Sources
Vitamins	Those which can be dissolved in fats are called fat-soluble vitamins. Those which can be dissolved in water are called water-soluble vitamins. Most can't be manufactured by the body itself but must be absorbed from foods. Their function in the body can be likened to that of lubricating oil in machines. The following chart provides the various functions and food sources of various vitamins.	
1. Fat-soluble vitamins Vitamin A	1. Enables the eyes to adjust to darkness; maintains normal vision (particularly night vision). 2. Protects the epidermis and mucous membranes from bacterial invasion (aids in resistance against infection). 3. Promotes the normal growth of teeth and bones.	Liver, egg yolk, milk, yogurt, butter, yellow/green vegetables and fruits (such as cabbage, carrots, spinach, tomatoes, papaya, mango, etc.), cod liver oil, potatoes with yellow or red center.
Vitamin D	1. Aids the absorption and use of calcium and phosphorus. 2. Helps the normal development of teeth and bones. 3. Provides the physiological necessities of nerves and muscles.	Cod liver oil, egg yolk,, yogurt, fish, liver, milk with added Vitamin D.
Vitamin E	1. Reduces the oxidation of Vitamin A and polyunsaturated fatty acids; controls the oxidation of cells. 2. Maintains the function of the animal reproductive system.	Grains, rice bran oil, wheat germ oil, cottonseed oil, green leafy vegetables, egg yolk, nuts.
Vitamin K	Aids the formation of thrombin which is a substance required in the clotting of blood; prevents continuous bleeding.	Green leafy vegetables such as spinach and lettuce are the best sources of Vitamin K. Egg yolk and liver also contain a small amount.
2. Water-soluble vitamins Vitamin B1	1. Increases the appetite. 2. Promotes the movement of intestines and the secretion of digestive liquids. 3. Prevents and cures Beriberi as well as Neuritis. 4. Promotes animal growth. 5. Has carbohydrate oxidizing function.	Germinated rice, malt, rice bran, liver, lean meat, yeast, beans, egg yolk, fish eggs, vegetables, etc.
Vitamin B2	1. Helps oxidation and the reduction process of cells. 2. Prevents blood vessels in the eyes from filling with blood and the edges of one's mouth from cracking and hurting.	Yeast, viscera, milk, eggs, peanuts, beans, green leafy vegetables, lean meat, etc.
Vitamin B6	1. Is a type of coenzyme which helps the synthesis and hydrolysis of amino acids. 2. Helps 'colored' amino acids to become nicotinic acid.	Meat, fish, vegetables, yeast, malt, liver, kidney, unpolished rice, eggs, milk, beans, peanuts, etc.
Vitamin B12	1. Promotes the synthesis of nucleic acid. 2. Has important function for the metabolism of carbohydrates and fats, and influences the thickness of glutathione in the blood. 3. Cures pernicious anemia and nervous system damage caused by pernicious anemia.	Liver, kidney, lean meat, milk, cheese, egg, etc.
Niacin (Nicotinic Acid)	1. Forms the essential ingredients of two coenzymes in the carbohydrate dissolving process. The main function of these coenzymes is the transport of hydrogen. 2. Makes the skin healthy and benefits the nervous system.	Liver, yeast, unpolished rice, all grain products, lean meat, eggs, fish, dried bean curd, green leafy vegetables, milk.etc.
Folacin (Folic Acid)	1. Helps the production of red and white blood cells; prevents Pernicious anemia. 2. Promotes the synthesis of nucleic acid and nucleic protein.	Fresh green vegetables, liver, kidney, lean meat, etc.
Vitamin C	1. Helps the formation of collagen; enables cells to preserve healthy form. 2. Speeds up the healing process. 3. Increases resistance against contagious diseases.	Dark green and yellow/red vegetables, fruits (such as green peppers, guavas, citrus, tomatoes, lemon, etc.)

The most essential function of the thyroid gland is the increase in metabolism and moderation of the body's functions. Furthermore, the main ingredient of the thyroid gland is iodine. If iodine is lacking in the diet, the body's cellular oxidation and basic metabolic rate (the energy required for such activities as maintaining body temperature, digestion, breathing, etc.) will be affected; Furthermore, the thyroid gland maintains regular metabolism, and it swells when the body works to an excessive degree. By eating more foods which contain iodine (sea plants such as seaweed, black moss, nori etc.) one can prevent swelling of the thyroid gland.

令您賞心悅目的叢書
A SERIES OF BOOKS FOR YOUR PLEASURE AND ENJOYMENT

Chinese Cuisine

204頁 / 204pages
180道菜 / 180recipes
中文版 / 中英對照
C、C&E ＊●

Chinese Cooking

104頁 / 104pages
89道菜 / 89recipes
中、英文版 / C,E
＊

Chinese Seafood

120頁 / 104pages
161道菜 / 127recipes
中、英文版 / C,E
＊

簡餐專輯
CHINESE ONE DISH MEALS

104頁 / 104pages
47道菜 / 47recipes
中英對照 / C&E
＊

點心專輯
CHINESE SNACKS Revised

100頁 / 100pages
98道菜 / 98recipes
中英對照 / C&E
＊

中國菜(第二冊)
CHINESE CUISINE (II)
WEI-CHUAN'S COOK BOOK

280pages / 280pages
187道菜 / 237recipes
中英對照 / C&E
●

悅目美揷花
MEDITATIONS ON NATURE
THE ART OF FLOWER ARRANGEMENT

184頁 / 184pages
90種花藝 / 90types
中英對照 / C&E
＊

健康食譜
Healthful Cooking

120頁 / 120pages
100道菜 / 100recipes
中英對照 / C&E
＊

家常菜 豪華版

200頁 / 200pages
226道菜 / 226recipes
中文版 / C

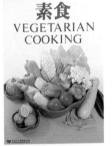

素食
VEGETARIAN COOKING

116頁 / 116pages
84道菜 / 84recipes
中英對照 / C&E
＊●

均衡飲食
LOW-CHOLESTEROL CHINESE CUISINE

128頁 / 128pages
99道菜 / 99recipes
中英對照 / C&E
＊

拼盤與盤飾 CHINESE
APPETIZERS & GARNISHES

160頁 / 160pages
164道盤飾 / 164recipes
中英對照 / C&E
＊●

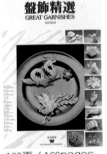

盤飾精選
GREAT GARNISHES

160頁 / 160pages
158道盤飾 / 158recipes
中英對照 / C&E
＊

CHINESE GARNISHES II
Curving Technique

CHINESE GARNISHES I
Striking Flowers

盤飾錄影帶
Videos For Garnishes

雕花刀
Carving Tools

日本料理
JAPANESE CUISINE

104pages
71recipes
C&E

微波爐食譜
Microwave Cooking Chinese Style

112頁 / 112pages
62道菜 / 62recipes
中英對照 / C&E
＊●

Chinese Style II
微波爐食譜
Microwave Cooking

128頁 / 128pages
76道菜 / 76recipes
中英對照 / C&E
＊●

基礎算術
TRANSITION MATH

I KNOW IT! BOOK

　　由味全出版社與美國
School Zone Publish-
ing 合作出版的中英文
對照兒童叢書是小朋友
學習英文、數學、圖案
和色彩等知識的最佳工
具，篇篇生動有趣，能
充分享受在遊戲中學習
的樂趣。
內容包涵：

幼兒學習系列：①連線遊戲②形狀③色彩遊戲

兒童學習系列：①閱讀訓練②基礎算數③學習
　　　　　　　　1－10

趣味學習系列：①我會讀②趣味遊戲③數數看

paperbound　　●精裝本hardbound　　C&E：Chinese & English bilingual edition

均衡飲食

味全食譜　版權所有

局版台業字第0179號
定價：新台幣 280 元

印刷：喬茂印刷製版有限公司
地址：台北市環河北路一段103號2樓　電話：5527612－4